PENTECOST I

Interpreting the Lessons of the Church Year

Terence E. Fretheim

PENTECOST 1

PROCLAMATION 6 | SERIES C

FORTRESS PRESS | MINNEAPOLIS

PROCLAMATION 6
Interpreting the Lessons of the Church Year
Series C, Pentecost 1

Copyright © 1997 Augsburg Fortress. All rights reserved. Except for brief quotations in critical articles or reviews, no part of this book may be reproduced in any manner without prior written permission of the publisher. Write to: Augsburg Fortress, 426 S. Fifth St., Box 1209, Minneapolis, MN 55440.

Scripture quotations, from the New Revised Standard Version Bible, copyright © 1989 by the Division of Christian Education of the National Council of Churches in the U.S.A. and are used by permission.

Cover design: Ellen Maly
Text design: David Lott

The Library of Congress has cataloged the first four volumes of Series A as follows:

Proclamation 6, Series A: interpreting the lessons of the church
    year.
        p.   cm.
    Contents: [1] Advent/Christmas / J. Christiaan Beker — [2]
Epiphany / Susan K. Hedahl — [3] Lent / Peter J. Gomes — [4] Holy
Week / Robin Scroggs.
    ISBN 0-8006-4207-4 (v. 1 : alk. paper) — ISBN 0-8006-4208-2 (v.
2 : alk. paper) — ISBN 0-8006-4209-0 (v. 3 : alk. paper) — ISBN 0-8006-4210-4
(v. 4 : alk. paper).
    1. Bible—Homiletical use. 2. Bible—liturgical lessons,
English.
BS534.5P74 1995
251—dc20   95-4622
                                                                               CIP

    Series C:
    Advent/Christmas / E. Elizabeth Johnson—ISBN 0-8006-4231-7
    Epiphany / Richard I. Pervo—ISBN 0-8006-4232-5
    Lent / Bernhard W. Anderson —ISBN 0-8006-4233-3
    Holy Week / Patricia Wilson-Kastner—ISBN 0-8006-4234-1
    Easter / L. William Countryman—ISBN 0-8006-4235-X
    Pentecost 1 / Terence E. Fretheim—ISBN 0-8006-4236-8
    Pentecost 2 / James L. Boyce—ISBN 0-8006-4237-6
    Pentecost 3 / William L. Holladay—ISBN 0-8006-4238-4

The paper used in this publication meets the minimum requirements of American National Standard for Information Sciences—Permanence of Paper for Printed Library Materials, ANSI Z329.48-1948.

Manufactured in the U. S. A.   AF 1-4236

    01   00   99   98   97   1   2   3   4   5   6   7   8   9   10

Contents

Pentecost Sunday *The Day of Pentecost/Whitsunday*	7
First Sunday after Pentecost *The Holy Trinity/Trinity Sunday*	14
Second Sunday after Pentecost *Ninth Sunday in Ordinary Time/Proper 4*	20
Third Sunday after Pentecost *Tenth Sunday in Ordinary Time/Proper 5*	27
Fourth Sunday after Pentecost *Eleventh Sunday in Ordinary Time/Proper 6*	33
Fifth Sunday after Pentecost *Twelfth Sunday in Ordinary Time/Proper 7*	41
Sixth Sunday after Pentecost *Thirteenth Sunday in Ordinary Time/Proper 8*	48
Seventh Sunday after Pentecost *Fourteenth Sunday in Ordinary Time/Proper 9*	55
Eighth Sunday after Pentecost *Fifteenth Sunday in Ordinary Time/Proper 10*	62
Ninth Sunday after Pentecost *Sixteenth Sunday in Ordinary Time/Proper 11*	70

Pentecost Sunday
The Day of Pentecost/Whitsunday

Lectionary	First Lesson	Psalm	Second Lesson	Gospel
Revised Common	Acts 2:1-21 or Gen. 11:1-9	Ps. 104:24-34, 35b	Rom. 8:14-17 or Acts 2:1-21	John 14:8-17, (25-27)
Episcopal (BCP)	Acts 2:1-11 or Joel 2:28-32	Ps. 104:25-32 (-37) or 33:12-15, 18-22	1 Cor. 12:4-13 or Acts 2:1-11	John 20:19-23 or John 14:8-17
Roman Catholic	Acts 2:1-11	Ps. 104:1, 24, 29-31, 34	Rom. 8:8-17	John 14:15-16, 23b-26
Lutheran (LBW)	Gen. 11:1-9	Ps. 104:25-34	Acts 2:1-21	John 15:26-27; 16:4b-11

The Bible reader may wonder what is so special about Pentecost. After all, the Spirit is active throughout Old Testament times, indeed from the creation, and is recognized as such (Gen. 1:2; Isa. 63:10). Luke himself, from the very beginning of his Gospel (1:15, 41, 67), refers to certain people being filled with the Spirit. Yet, several differences can be cited. One difference, recognized in the remarkable inclusivity of the texts in Joel and Acts, is the democratization of the gifts of the Spirit. The Spirit moves beyond leaders to catch up all people of faith in all of their diversity. Second, Pentecost issues in a new kind of intensity of the Spirit's presence; the Spirit is active in a newly pervasive way in the community of faith. Finally, the work of the Spirit relates specifically to Jesus Christ, his life, death, and resurrection. The Spirit mediates the teaching and work of Christ to the world.

FIRST LESSON: GENESIS 11:1-9

As elsewhere in Genesis 1–11, this text is a typical story of humankind ("whole earth"), not a reflection on a specific event. All human beings speak the same language, with a common vocabulary. As a single community, they migrate to the east and settle in Shinar (Babylonia). This community is scattered from this one place (Babel) and various peoples emerge who speak different languages (10:5, 20, 31—the Table of Nations—cover this same reality from another perspective). The text could be read as a critique of royal building programs or a judgment on the pride of nations. The story, however, is remarkably democratic, reinforcing the view that the problem here is generally human.

The text is symmetrically structured, wherein the situation of vv. 1-4 is reversed in vv. 6-9. The direct speech of the peoples' plans in vv. 3-4 parallels that of God's plans in consultation with the divine council in vv. 6-7 ("come, let us"). Between these segments is God's decision to conduct an inquiry (v. 5), the story's turning point. That God and the humans are not in dialogue with each other is one of the most ominous elements in this text.

The precise nature of the builders' failure remains elusive. The building of a city with a tower *as such* is not pernicious. The issue is not that they build or what they build. The effort to secure a home seems natural enough, and the builders raise no God issues. Even the tower may not be an issue. It is a city tower or a temple tower (ziggurat), a stepped, mountain-shaped structure. In Babylonian culture, the latter was the vehicle for communication between earthly and heavenly realms through priestly mediation. The phrase, "its top in the heavens," was popularly used of ziggurats and too much is made of it. The text is unlikely to carry theories about a storming of heaven or usurping the place of God.

The objective of "making a name (*sem*) for ourselves" is a more fruitful direction. This may signal an attempt to secure the future by one's own efforts, particularly in view of 12:2, where God is the subject of accrued renown. The name they actually receive—Babel (confusion)—ironically testifies to the futility of their efforts. Yet, the desire for fame does not seem reprehensible enough *in and of itself* to occasion the magnitude of the divine response.

The basic human failure is seen in the motivation, "otherwise we shall be scattered abroad," as is clear from the moral order talk; the crime corresponds precisely to God's judgment (vv. 8-9). The issue is anxiety and insecurity about the future, a fear of not keeping their community intact in the face of a threatening world. Only because of this do other objectives become problematic. The building projects constitute a bid to secure a future as a unified community, isolated from the rest of the world.

This move constitutes a challenge to God's command to fill the earth (1:28); but, even more, it occasions a divine concern for the creation, for only in scattering can human beings fulfill their charge to be caretakers of the earth (see 1:28). Efforts focused narrowly on the future of the human community is a self-preserving, isolationist view of the world and places the rest of creation in jeopardy. The building thus *understeps* rather than oversteps human limits, for it is *not* scattering that puts the creation at risk.

God's response focuses, not on the project, but on *other* possibilities of united human endeavor (v. 6); it is thus a preventive measure. The *unity* of humankind so conceived could promote other projects that place the creation in jeopardy. God's response is judgmental but is also in the interests of the future of "all the earth" (vv. 8-9). God makes the languages so diffuse that they have to establish separate linguistic communities. The confusing that leads to the scattering is thus a means to another end: the filling of and caring for the earth in fulfillment of the creational command. Though the text is not antiurban, it does recognize that human progress of whatever sort is never unaccompanied by sin and its potential for disaster.

The text presents a complex view of unity and diversity. Ordinarily, unity in the human community is regarded as being in tune with God's purposes. But here, because the unity desired stands over against the divine will to spread abroad, God must resist it. Those who seek to save life will lose it. The right kind of unity is present only when the community manifests a concern for the entire creation. Diversity is part of God's intention for the world, as is evident from the marvelously pluriform character of God's creation. In tune with those intentions, God makes a decisive move here on behalf of diversity and difference. God will promote diversity at the expense of any form of unity that seeks to preserve itself in isolation from the rest of the creation.

A contemporary parallel may be seen in the often isolated way in which the church relates to the world. In the interests of unity and preserving its own future, Christians often stay close to home and don't risk venturing forth. The command of Matt. 28:18-20 is a call for the church to scatter across the face of the earth. If the church refuses this call, God may enter into judgment against the church and find a way of getting them beyond their own clique out into the world on behalf of the creation. The unity of the church is not to be found by focusing on unity, building churches and programs that present a unified front before the temptations of the world. True unity finally is a gift, to be found in those things that are not tangible or centered on one's own self-interests. Unity will be forged most successfully in taking on the task of getting beyond one's own kind on behalf of the word in the world.

Different languages are probably more blessing than bane, more gift than problem. They enrich people's understanding of the world. More generally, speaking and hearing are a more complex reality, and include truly hearing "the other" in various life situations. Difficulties in communication can often lead to difficulties in relationships, but this usually has more to do with the failings of people who seek to communicate than to differences in languages.

SECOND LESSON: ACTS 2:1-21

The flow of the narrative in Acts 2 moves from an abruptly introduced story of the gift of the Spirit at a celebration of the Jewish feast of Pentecost (2:1-

13), to Peter's sermon on the significance of this event, in which Joel 2:28-32 is the central text (2:14-36), to the overwhelmingly positive response from the hearers (2:37-41). The pericope cuts off in the middle of the sermon, and the interpreter would be wise to be attentive to the entire story in thinking through its import.

The abruptness of the introduction matches the appearance of the wind and the fire. These phenomena recall Old Testament texts, associated either with the Spirit of God (the Hebrew *ruach* can be translated either wind or spirit) or the intense presence of God. Luke may have Gen. 1:2 in mind, as he reflects on Pentecost in terms of God's new creation, but also Gen. 8:1, where God's wind moves the flooded creation to a newly ordered world. The association of fire with God's intense presence is no doubt important, but the explicit link is made with the fire of Joel 2 and the promise of the gift of the Spirit. An Old Testament connection is also seen in Isa. 66:15, 18, which link fire and a gathering of "nations of every language," who "shall come and see my glory." Isaiah goes on to speak of the proclamation of God's glory in the hearing of "distant coastlands"; a listing of the nations who hear in Isa. 66:19 is mirrored in the even more extensive listing of the nations in Acts 2:9-11.

The Spirit is God's gift for mission, which can only be carried out through the scattering of the people from Judea and Jerusalem back into their own nations throughout the world. This "scattering" recalls the Babel story, where God's purposes in creation are accomplished through filling the earth, not gathering together among one's own kind. That the Spirit comes upon devout Jews from "every nation under heaven"(!) also links back to the creation story, as well as to the "all flesh" of Joel 2, as the universality of the gift of the Spirit is stressed. The Spirit is not a gift for just a few leaders in Jerusalem. The Spirit is God's gift for the world, which means that the Spirit cannot be controlled by a chosen few or confined within certain "churchly" boundaries (a tendency through the centuries). This democratization of the gift is also evident in the language of inclusivity (men and women, young and old; 2:17), which recalls the equality of "male and female" in Gen. 1:27 and the remarkable diversity of God's creation.

The references to cosmic phenomena in Joel (Acts 2:19-20) also recall creation motifs. They also show that some elements in the prophecy are understood not to have been literally fulfilled. The interest is not to show how each cosmic reference corresponds to phenomena that occurred at Pentecost. The interpreter is not, for example, to look for specific matters that might fulfill the references to a bloody moon or a darkened sun. The focus of fulfillment is the gift of the Spirit, and these cosmic references are witness in a nonspecific way to the universal effects of the gift of the

Spirit on the entire creation. These phenomena usher in "the day of the Lord" (Acts 2:20). This phrase recalls another Old Testament tradition. Themes of both judgment and salvation are present in the reference to the "day of the Lord," often anticipated in Old Testament texts with metaphoric language about fire and darkness and clouds and blood. These prophecies include judgment on God's own people (the fall of Samaria [Amos 5:18-20] and Jerusalem [Zeph. 1:14-18]) or on the enemies of the righteous (Isa. 66:15-16; Mal. 4:1-3). The latter texts are most pertinent here. They connect well with the reference to the "remnant" in the Joel text (Joel 2:32) that immediately follows the end of the quotation in Acts. On the day of the Lord, of which the gift of the Spirit is a part, the enemies of God's people will be destroyed and those who call on the name of the Lord (the righteous remnant) shall be saved. The salvation to be experienced centers on salvation from the effects of the oppressive sins of other people (as in the exodus from Egypt), not from salvation from their own sins. The salvation envisaged is comprehensive in scope.

Both the speaking and the hearing in the text are important. The gift of the Spirit not only issues in the inspired speech of the participants, but also in an inspired hearing on their part. The speaking is not a "speaking in tongues," but a speaking in their own native languages (vv. 6, 11), which would be intelligible to those whose language it is. The most basic issue is not a unity of language, but a unity of message regarding "the mighty acts of God" (v. 11). An inspired hearing is evident in that each of the peoples present hears the one Gospel in their native tongue.

Thus the gift of the Spirit does not remove the diversity of languages; indeed, this gift results in a linguistic cacophony. But the essential content of the speaking is the same, namely, the Gospel. This is the gift of a new hearing that transcends language barriers, a new commonality in understanding God's work in Jesus. Acts 2 speaks of the enabling of people who speak various languages to hear and understand the one Gospel for all the earth.

GOSPEL: JOHN 14:8-17, (23b-27)

This segment is part of the farewell discourses of Jesus to his disciples in John 13:31—17:26, which interpret the passion narratives that follow. More narrowly, this text is part of the discourse in chap. 14, marked off by the exhortation, "let not your hearts be troubled" (14:1, 27). The context for such a comforting word is Jesus' announced departure (13:33) and the disciples' questioning of Jesus' leaving "home" (13:36-37; 14:5, 8-9, 22).

Jesus' words respond to specific questions, which may reflect those of early Christians to which the Gospel of John is in part a response. The way in which Jesus handles the questions would be an interesting approach to take to the text. His responses range from return questions to mild rebuke to wonderment about claims being made to reassurances. Jesus' responsive words center on the relationships between Jesus and God the Father and Jesus and the Holy Spirit. These relationships with God and Spirit mean that Jesus' departure is not like the departure of others in their experience. God is already present in what Jesus says and does (14:10-11) and will continue to be so in the work of the Spirit. This is not simply a presence "with," but a presence "in" (14:17) and hence a presence to the entire person. The presence of God will not simply be coextensive with Jesus in the flesh, and hence it is an advantage for the disciples that Jesus departs.

The disciples will be able to count on God's presence, but God will also send the Spirit to be their *paraclete*, that is, one who "stands beside" them to be their comforter, advocate, and teacher (the texts from John 15–16 fill out the role of the Spirit; cf. Rom. 8:14-17). As Jesus has related to them during his earthly life, so will the Spirit now be "another" paraclete for them, continuing the ministry of Jesus in their midst. From John's perspective (see 20:19-23), the Spirit is given directly by Jesus to the disciples. The Pentecost event is thus seen as an extension of the gift of the Spirit to other followers of Jesus and in a more public way.

The disciples' questioning is not unlike that of many people of faith who, especially in times of sickness or oppression or death, wonder about various matters, from the presence of God with them to the destiny of those who may depart or already have. It may be difficult for many such persons to believe that God's presence in the Spirit is as real as that of the presence of a flesh-and-blood human being. Many would prefer a voice they can actually hear and a body they can actually touch (cf. Thomas in 20:24-29 on not seeing, seeing, and believing). The disciples are assured that even their questions, when asked in Jesus' name, will be addressed (14:13-14) when Jesus is no longer present to respond to them. Just as Jesus has been their teacher, so will the Spirit be (14:26), and that teaching will be consonant with what Jesus is now telling them.

The promised peace is not to be identified with the usual peace of which the world speaks (14:27), which is often defined in psychological terms or as the absence of war or conflict. It may be that the disciples will experience deep and debilitating conflicts. It may be that persons of faith will suffer profoundly from personal violence or illness. In either case, we may not fully know "peace" as it is commonly defined among us. But a peace that God gives can be a reality even for us, and it may not be entirely different from the kind of peace understood in worldly terms. Peace may take various forms. Perhaps it is a confidence that we are loved by God, or a deep sense that God is present and at work in our lives and our world even though it does not appear to be the case. Such peace may come in and through the ministrations of Jesus' disciples, whose lives are to be shaped in such a way as to "keep my word" (14:23-24) and "keep my commandments" (14:15, 21). The ministry of such persons will give the Holy Spirit "body" in the midst of whatever troubles may come our way. Such a ministry, defined as "doing the works that I do" (14:12), will be even more extensive ("greater") than that of Jesus. The text from 1 Cor. 12:4-13 speaks of such articulate and bodily forms that the Spirit assumes among us in persons of faith.

First Sunday after Pentecost
The Holy Trinity/Trinity Sunday

Lectionary	First Lesson	Psalm	Second Lesson	Gospel
Revised Common	Prov. 8:1-4, 22-31	Psalm 8	Rom. 5:1-5	John 16:12-15
Episcopal (BCP)	Isa. 6:1-8	Psalm 29 or Cant. 2 or 13	Rev. 4:1-11	John 16:(5-11), 12-15
Roman Catholic	Prov. 8:22-31	Ps. 8:3-9	Rom. 5:1-5	John 16:12-15
Lutheran (LBW)	Prov. 8:22-31	Psalm 8	Rom. 5:1-5	John 16:12-15

The understanding of the Trinity is not fully developed in the Bible; that awaits postbiblical conciliar decisions. Yet, this later development of the doctrine of the Trinity is enabled by key biblical texts. The most obvious biblical foundations are those New Testament texts which speak of Father, Son, and Holy Spirit (for instance, Matt. 28:19) and Johannine conceptions of the Logos and the Spirit. The Old Testament also prepares the way. The text about Wisdom from Proverbs 8, especially when coupled with Gen. 1:2 and 1:26 ("let us"), give clear evidence of a social understanding of God and the richness and complexity of the divine realm. God is not in heaven alone, but is engaged in a relationship of mutuality within the divine realm, and chooses to share the creative process with others within that realm. That human beings are created specifically as a result of this dialogical divine activity gives them a special place, for they are in the image of a God who creates in a way that shares power with others. The wise human being is one who will use these creative powers responsibly and with integrity.

Trinity Sunday provides an occasion for a more didactic form of preaching. We all need further instruction about God!

FIRST LESSON: PROVERBS 8:22-31

Proverbs 8 consists of a discourse by wisdom, personified as a woman (see 1:20-33). In 8:1-5 she takes up a position at life's crossroads, and presents herself as a teacher of the virtues to the immature. Wisdom's description of herself is actually a description of the individual who would be wise. In vv. 6-9 she expresses the character of her speech, that is, the speech of a wise person—truthful, righteous, straightforward, sincere. In vv. 10-11 she commends the unsurpassable value of the virtues that follow in vv. 12-21—prudence, humility, discretion, insight, diligence, fear of the Lord, hatred of evil, wise counsel, love of wisdom, integrity of speech, justice and righteousness in leadership and daily life. All these virtues, to be cultivated and embodied by one who would be wise, carry their own reward in a life well lived. The chapter concludes (vv. 32-36) with another invitation to a wise life and, it follows, a joy-filled life. Listening for wisdom, keeping its ways, watching and waiting for wisdom, is the key to life rather than death. Whoever finds wisdom "finds life." The fear of the Lord is the *beginning* of wisdom, but it is only the beginning.

Proverbs 8 now moves from wisdom in terms of a description of human character to wisdom as the character of the entire creation (vv. 22-31). Wisdom was created by God before anything else, at the very beginning, before the external world was brought into being. It is remarkable that the language of conception and birthing is so prominent in this description of wisdom. Evident particularly in the "bringing forth" of vv. 24-25, it may also be present in the "created" (or conceived) of v. 22 and the "set up" (or woven together—see Ps. 139:13) of v. 23. God is viewed as the mother of wisdom; creation is conceived in maternal terms. Because that which is birthed, namely wisdom, is also conceived in female terms, means that there is an especially close correlation between wisdom and God. Wisdom too has her children, and human beings are included among them (v. 31). Wisdom also may be described as a "little child" (see NRSV footnote to v. 30), in whom God the parent delights. The creation of wisdom, and all else in God's good creation, is described in terms filled with joy and playfulness (see Job 38:7).

As such, wisdom is primordial and without parallel in her relationship to God—and hence of unsurpassable standing in God's world. All the creating that follows is shaped in terms of already-created wisdom. This means that wisdom is the fundamental character of all of God's creation; anywhere one looks in creation—mountains, seas, springs of water, sky, fields, the inhabited world, including the humans—one sees evidence of wisdom. The joy-filled character of wisdom, evident from the very beginning and hence descriptive of every aspect of God's creational activity (vv. 30-31), becomes in turn a fundamental description of the wise life (vv. 32-36).

Wisdom was the decisive factor in God's shaping of the entire created order, from the nonhuman creation to the community to the individual human character (see 3:19-20). Even more, wisdom is, by God's designs and actions, built into the very structures of the world order. Hence, the person who is wise will live a life that is in tune with all of God's creation. Such persons will "fit in" to God's world; their lives will correspond to the very character of God's creation and hence individual and community life will be "very good," characterized by beauty, joy, peace, and well-being.

Because wisdom is built into the very structures of God's good creation, it is accessible to all creatures. Knowledge of the character of wisdom, and hence knowledge of God, can be discerned by all who carefully observe God's creation, though finally it is beyond human comprehension. But wisdom is not simply a static reality. Its personification means that it is dynamic, reaching out to human beings and inviting them to participate in the larger sphere of wisdom characteristic of God's entire creation.

This personification of wisdom goes beyond a simple literary device for depicting a divine attribute. As that which is created, it stands in some independence from God, with a life of her own. Just how this figure is understood in Proverbs is uncertain, but over time it lends itself to being conceived as a heavenly being standing alongside God and participating with God in the creation of the world (see Wisdom 7:2—8:1). Thereby, the Godhead is conceived in social and interrelational terms. Wisdom would thus be parallel to the Creator Spirit of Gen. 1:2 (see the "us" in 1:26), and it informs the Logos language of John 1:1-4. These connections make this an especially appropriate text for Trinity Sunday.

SECOND LESSON: ROMANS 5:1-5

What a profusion of key words are strung together in only five verses: justification, faith, peace, grace, love, hope, glory, and suffering. All are linked to the work of God through the other persons of the Trinity: God through Jesus Christ; God through the Holy Spirit. The Christ who died for us proves *God's* love for us (v. 8); the Holy Spirit is a gift to pour out *God's* love into our hearts (v. 5). Note the key place given to love here. God is not divided within the divine self; love identifies the relationship of the Father, the Son, and the Holy Spirit. Through the actions of this divine love, we are caught up into the depths of the inner-divine relationship. That love shown in Christ is poured out from God through the Spirit. To us! Into *our* hearts! God is love and we are now embraced within that love.

Because of this work of God, we have been justified by faith. We have peace with God. We have been given ongoing access to God's grace; indeed, we stand within that grace. We have had the love of God poured into our hearts. We have hope for the future. All of these gifts have been lavished upon us by this God. The result is reconciliation—while we were sinners. Nothing now stands between us and God. All these gifts of God engender hope for the future in the midst of the worst the world can throw our way. Because of who we have now become, and the vocation to which we have been called, sufferings of various sorts will certainly come our way. But not every suffering will produce endurance and character and hope, even for the most devout of Christian folk. The sufferings in view are those associated with the vocation to which we have been called (for Paul's sufferings, 2 Cor. 11:16-29; see 1 Peter 2:21). In all the ins and outs of this vocation, God is at work effecting that which is good, for us and for others. This divine work in our lives is not confined to the past. The ongoing work of the Holy Spirit catches us up into the love of God and engenders a hope in us that can strengthen us in the midst of suffering. The promise here is not the removal of suffering from life, a trouble-free vocation. The promise is God's loving presence at work within that suffering so that it does not lead finally to disappointment and despair.

Given this profound reality, we will not boast in anything that we have done, but we will boast in the Lord (v. 11; cf. 1 Cor. 1:29-31). And we will boast in the hope that someday God will be all in all (v. 2). And, because of this hope, we may even boast in our sufferings. But this is not a boasting in our own strengths or abilities to endure sufferings, as if people would now think more highly of us because of what we have been able to do. This is a boasting of our weaknesses, that is, a boldness in the midst of such suffering, because of what Christ is able to accomplish in and through us. When we are weak, Christ and Christ's power is able to be more visible to others in us; we ourselves will not get so much in the way of the one to whom we witness. Others will then be able to look at us and see, not our own talents and abilities, but God in Christ. Because of this greater transparency, when we are weak, then we are strong (2 Cor. 12:1-10).

GOSPEL: JOHN 16:12-15

This text is one more segment from Jesus' farewell discourse to his disciples that focuses on the gift of the Spirit. This passage makes especially clear that talk about the Spirit cannot be separated from Jesus and his ministry. The work of the Spirit has to do with the work of the other persons of the Trinity. This text is revealing of a fundamental character of the Trinity, namely, God is a social reality. The relationships within the Godhead are important for how one understands the work of the Spirit. The Holy Spirit does not function independently of the Father and the Son; the Spirit is not a freewheeling reality, out and about in the world "doing his own thing." The Spirit will "speak what he hears" from the inner-divine conversation. Negatively, the Spirit will not stand at odds with anything that the disciples have seen and heard in Jesus. Positively, what Jesus has said and done will not get lost, but will be reinforced and confirmed in the Spirit's work.

The remarkable testimony here is that the inner-divine relationship and conversation catches up the disciples into that reality. It is as if the disciples are present in the very throne room of God and overhear that inner-divine conversation, not unlike the way in which the prophets were brought in on the deliberations of the divine council (see Jer. 23:18-24). Jesus does not want to keep the disciples ignorant of what God is about in the world (see Gen. 18:17; Amos 3:7). For Jesus, a lack of the knowledge of God on the part of the disciples—or us—is not a virtue.

At the same time, it is made clear that there is more to be heard from God than was evident in Jesus' ministry. Understandings that the disciples do not now have will be filled out through the work of the Spirit. An *ongoing* inner-divine conversation will shape the work of the Spirit. Jesus had "much more to tell," but the disciples could not take it all in during their time with Jesus. The Spirit will continue to guide the community of faith into "all the truth." This work of the Spirit will *extend* the truth regarding what God has been doing in Jesus and will be doing in the future ("things that are to come"). This "truth" is not to be identified with Jesus himself in a narrow way, but everything with which Jesus has to do as the supreme revelation of God. The truth here is understood in fundamentally relational terms, but that does not exclude matters of content. God has more truth to tell. And God will speak that truth in and through the Spirit, and the last time anyone looked we had not yet arrived. An example of such truth may be the development of early church reflection about the nature and work of the Trinity that, while especially present in these texts from John, moves beyond the New Testament conversation.

A common temptation of the disciples of Jesus will be that we think we have the entire truth about God already available, whether in the Scriptures or in the subsequently developed tradition, and all we have to do is package it right and deliver it well. On the contrary, God is on the move with an ever-changing world, and as persons of faith we need to have our ears open for ever-new ways in which the Spirit is speaking truth to the church. Human questions are always on the move (see above on John 14) and God will be genuinely responsive. One of the basic gifts of the Spirit is discernment, and that entails a deep level of listening so that we can sort out well the truth from amid the cacophony of voices heard in our time claiming that they have the truth about God.

One of the intriguing results of such listening is that the truth of God and the world not only becomes more fully understood, but increasingly more interesting. The word about God spoken by we who are disciples is often boring because we are all too often satisfied with the truth about God that we presently have in hand and are not sufficiently attuned to voice of the Spirit. One of the key gifts of the Spirit is creative imagination, leading the people of God into ever-new vistas of the knowledge of God. Among the failures of the church is a failure of the imagination. I suspect that one of the first statements that persons of faith will make when they no longer see in a glass darkly but face to face will be, *That's really interesting!*

In discerning the truth about God and thinking it through, it becomes apparent that the more we know, the more we know we do not know. As such, one result of such a learning process under the guidance of the Spirit is that God becomes more and more of a mystery. The depth and inexhaustibility of God and God's ways in the world become more and more apparent. It follows that the less we know, the *less* of a mystery God is. And so, if we are protective of the present levels of our knowledge of God or cut off exploratory theological work and creative imaginings, we may not only stifle the work of the Spirit in leading us into all the truth, we will also reduce the divine mystery.

Second Sunday after Pentecost
Ninth Sunday in Ordinary Time/Proper 4

Lectionary	First Lesson	Psalm	Second Lesson	Gospel
Revised Common	I Kgs. 18:20-21, (22-29), 30-39 or 8:22-23, 41-43	Psalm 96 or 96:1-9	Gal. 1:1-12	Luke 7:1-10
Episcopal (BCP)	I Kgs. 8:22-23, 27-30, 41-43	Psalm 96 or 96:1-9	Gal. 1:1-10	Luke 7:1-10
Roman Catholic	I Kgs. 8:41-43	Ps. 117:1-2	Gal. 1:1-2, 6-10	Luke 7:1-10
Lutheran (LBW)	I Kgs. 8:(22-23, 27-30), 41-43	Psalm 117	Gal. 1:1-10	Luke 7:1-10

Christians are increasingly having to do with "the other," people unlike ourselves in varying ways who are moving into our neighborhoods. Inasmuch as mission is at the heart of who we are, relating to such outsiders is an obligation. How best to do so becomes a challenge. We know that certain extremes are to be avoided: retreating into a ghetto without genuine engagement, insisting that everyone "be like us," or an "inclusivism" that only celebrates differences and "anything goes." The instinct to preserve and conserve fights it out with the call to welcome the stranger and be open to new vistas that God might be opening before us. The need to watch for that which is dangerous to our personal or religious health contends with a need to recognize that God may be encountering us through the other. Some questions to ask: How do we experience the other? How does the other experience us? How do we experience *being* the other? How do we seriously take into account the voices of those who are different from ourselves? How might these others be a genuine gift of God to us? What in our traditions or practices is negotiable? What is nonnegotiable?

The Bible has resources for dealing with such questions as the people of God interact with various outsiders. The texts for this Sunday present us with three different encounters with outsiders, the foreigners in Solomon's prayer, the Judaizers with whom Paul contends, and a Roman centurion.

FIRST LESSON: I KINGS 8:22-23, 27-30, 41-43

This text is part of a lengthy prayer by Solomon (vv. 22-53) on the occasion of the dedication of the temple. The prayer is enclosed by Solomon's blessing of the assembly (vv. 14-21, 54-61) in which the fulfillment of God's promises to David and Moses is highlighted. The chapter as a whole is enclosed by liturgical actions (vv. 1-13, 62-66). The prayer itself is carefully shaped and formulated in such a way as to address the assembly (and their future life situations) as well as God. The introduction (vv. 22-26) centers on God's incomparability and God's keeping the Davidic covenant (see 2 Sam. 7:1-17) both now and into a future that reaches to the Babylonian exile (vv. 46-51). The conclusion (v. 53) focuses on God's promises to Moses (cf. v. 56). Thus, a two-pronged appeal to divine faithfulness to covenants at two major junctures in Israel's life opens and closes the prayer. God's faithfulness surrounds and grounds the petitions. Solomon and the people (vv. 30, 52) can pray in confidence because God is a promise-keeper. Because of the kind of God Israel's God is, they can pray knowing that their prayers will be heard and graciously acknowledged.

The next segment (vv. 27-30) constitutes a request that God hear the prayer and forgive in each of the cases that follow; this finds its parallel in v. 52, which adds God's eyes to the ears of God in v. 30. God is understood to be present and within "praying distance," dwelling both in heaven and in the temple (see Ps. 11:4). God's temple is here seen fundamentally in terms of a house of prayer. Yet, while God's people can lay claim to the promises, God's specific responses are not under the control of those who pray. God will answer prayer because God is gracious.

Seven petitions follow (vv. 31-32, 33-34, 35-36, 37-40, 41-43, 44-45, 46-50). Each petition anticipates future prayer situations faced by people, repeating the request for God to "hear in heaven" their prayers. A strong emphasis on God as a God who hears animates this text. All but the fifth petition, the one assigned for this Sunday, concern Israelites. The seventh petition relating to the people in exile is the most complete, perhaps reflecting the time of the prayer's final composition. All but the fifth and sixth petitions focus on sins the people have committed (less clearly in the fourth) and the importance of turning to God. Also stressed are the ill effects that sin has had on their lives. These adversities include personal, communal, and natural disasters. The prayer is not simply for God to forgive, but also for God to act to reverse the effects that their sins have had. Salvation is here understood to comprehend more than forgiveness of sin; it includes also the amelioration of the consequences of sin that have reverberated out into the larger community, including the natural order. This broader understanding of salvation is evident in the sixth petition, which concerns prayers in a time of battle.

The fifth petition (vv. 41-43) is unusual in this series in that it relates to foreigners who pray and it does not focus on a particular situation in life, whether of sin or adversity. The petition relates to anything concerning which the foreigner may offer prayer to God. The call is for God to hear and to act in response. Even such outsiders have access to God; they do not have to be integrated into the chosen community in order for their prayers to be heard and answered. Given the enclosing verses, this petition on behalf of foreigners is also grounded in God's promises to *Israel* and God's presence in Israel's temple. The faith of Israel is sufficiently "ecumenical" that it understands its God not only to be active in the lives of such outsiders but also to attend to their prayers (see Mal. 1:11). Also to be noted is the reference to the compassion of outsiders—Israel's captors—through whom God may work in response to Israel's prayers in captivity (vv. 46-50).

Solomon's petition can be related to various Old Testament texts that focus on foreigners. For example, the story of Elisha and Naaman (2 Kings 5; cf. Luke 4:27) speaks of a foreigner who is healed through the mediation of an Israelite prophet. Naaman moves from the healing to a confession of Israel's God as his Lord (2 Kgs. 5:15). This missional impact is precisely what animates Solomon's petition. Other pertinent texts are the story of Abraham and Abimelech (Genesis 20) and Isaiah's concern that the temple be "a house of prayer for all peoples" (Isa. 56:7; cf. Isa. 2:3; Ps. 47:9).

The foreigner of whom Solomon speaks may refer primarily to the numerous travelers who made their way through Israel. They have heard of Israel's God by reputation, namely, the great deeds done on behalf of Israel. This renown may draw some of these outsiders to the temple, where they offer prayer. Solomon gives God a good reason to answer their prayers: this could be key to drawing that person into the community of faith. Through answers to prayers, the foreigners would come to fear the Lord and realize that God's presence is indeed in this temple. Solomon returns to this missional theme more generally in the conclusion to his prayer (v. 60). The divine objective through Israel is that "all the peoples of the earth may know that the Lord is God."

The Gospel for this Sunday, Luke 7:1-10, accompanies this text because a Roman centurion—a foreigner—makes an appeal to Jesus, and Jesus responds not only with healing but with a recognition of his faith. In effect, *Jesus* responds to Solomon's petition!

SECOND LESSON: GALATIANS 1:1-10

Paul's letter to the Galatians will provide texts for the next six Sundays. The Galatians cannot certainly be identified, but were probably a people from central Asia Minor (Turkey), inhabiting a large swath of land through the middle of the country. Paul had traveled through this area during his second and third missionary journeys (Acts 16:6; 18:23), had been received well, and his preaching had converted many of these Gentiles to Christianity.

SECOND SUNDAY AFTER PENTECOST/PROPER 4

Paul wrote this letter about 55 C.E. while on his third journey, perhaps from Ephesus (western Turkey). The letter was occasioned by a visit of other missionaries to the Galatians, perhaps to be identified with Jewish Christians from Jerusalem (sometimes called Judaizers), who explicitly challenged Paul's interpretation of the Gospel. They preached "another gospel" than the one he had preached, a message that specified the observance of the Jewish law, including circumcision, on the part of Gentiles. Paul writes somewhat polemically regarding the trouble they have caused (see 1:8-9; 3:1; 5:12). He defends his authority as an apostle and stresses the sufficiency of faith in Jesus Christ for salvation, apart from law observance. Paul grounds salvation in Jesus' death and issues a clear statement of Christian freedom. The result is a sharp and succinct summary of Paul's understanding of the Christian faith and life. It is important to remember that such "legalistic" understandings are not characteristic of the Old Testament people, for whom obedience of law was never a means by which individuals entered into relationship with God. Such a perspective arose only among certain persons in post-Old Testament times.

This introduction to his letter (vv. 1-14) is similar to others, but contains several differences. In his typical greetings from others, he uniquely mentions "all" who are with him, thus giving additional weight to what follows. This letter does not just convey his own opinion. Moreover, with reference to attacks on his apostolicity, he stresses that he has been called, not by human beings, but by Christ and God. A concise statement of the faith follows: Christ has died "for our sins" by the will of God and thereby delivered us from the grasp of the present evil age (v. 4). This signals the heart of his message: this work of God in Christ is sufficient for their salvation; it needs no supplementation by certain forms of law observance, including circumcision.

With this ringing statement of the essence of the faith, Paul then replaces the typical thanksgiving (cf. 1 Cor. 1:4-9) with a sharp rebuke regarding the perversion of the gospel that has been put forth by these pretenders (vv. 6-10). This language is very strong, suggesting that the situation among the Galatians is at a critical stage. He perceives that only such a sharp word, repeated for emphasis, can get through to them the seriousness of their departure from the gospel he has preached. Indeed, this perverted word is so dangerous that, if it were allowed to prevail among them, it would result in their curse rather than their blessing.

Such a danger manifests itself in the church today whenever someone claims that, to be a Christian, faith in Jesus Christ must be supplemented by certain kinds of words and deeds. These extras added to the gospel (and commonly claimed to be a part of the gospel!) commonly take such forms as these: living a certain lifestyle; promoting certain values; being involved in certain kinds of social or political activities. The gospel can even be subtly perverted by speaking of such matters as "gospel imperatives." Such language dilutes the essence of the gospel word. The gospel is what *God* has done through the life and death of Jesus Christ; the gospel cannot be identified with anything that people do, however honorable and well intentioned. Any such extras pervert the gospel, endangering its very essence. And so Paul, while often tolerating diversity in a wide range of churchly thinking and practice, will tolerate absolutely no diversity here. The gospel is at stake, and so is our life and salvation.

GOSPEL: LUKE 7:1-10

Texts from the Gospel of Luke are once again picked up and continue through Pentecost. The texts for the Sundays in this volume are from Luke 7–10. A key transition point for Luke occurs in the middle of these chapters: "When the days drew near for him to be taken up, he set his face to go to Jerusalem" (9:51). This verse signals the beginning of Luke's story of Jesus' journey to Jerusalem; the story of his entry begins in 19:29.

The four texts to be considered prior to this transition (7:1-10; 7:11-17; 7:36—8:3; 8:26-39) conclude the section in Luke that focuses on Jesus' ministry in Galilee (begun at 4:14) and the concern to identify Jesus in various ways, including prophet and Messiah. This portrayal of Jesus' ministry includes a wide range of activities—preaching, teaching, healing, choosing, and preparing disciples. This activity and Jesus' growing popularity with the crowds begin to generate controversy with religious authorities. The section ends (9:7-50) by sounding ominous notes regarding the opposition to Jesus and announcements of his passion.

Luke 7:1-10 (parallels in Matt. 8:5-13 and John 4:46-53) follows the Sermon on the Plain (6:17-49). Jesus first encounters an outsider, a centurion, a Roman army officer in charge of one hundred foot soldiers (see 23:47). Luke's story of Cornelius the centurion in Acts 10, certainly related to Luke 7, constitutes Luke's story of the beginning of the mission to the Gentiles, and Luke 7 serves to ground that mission in Jesus' own ministry.

Jesus' ministry to Gentiles may in turn be grounded in the ministry of Israel's prophets. Note the parallels to the story of Naaman, another Gentile army commander (2 Kings 5). The following text (Luke 7:11-17) is linked to Elijah (1 Kings 17). Luke refers to these stories in 4:25-27 in connection with Jesus' reference to prophecy in terms of his own ministry (4:24). While "prophet" is not sufficient to identify Jesus, it is one key way in which Luke understands who Jesus is (see further at next Sunday's texts).

SECOND SUNDAY AFTER PENTECOST/PROPER 4

The character traits of the Roman army commander are noteworthy. He values his slave and seeks help for him. He is esteemed by the religious leaders of the area because of his love for the Jewish people and his support of their community through building a synagogue (similarly Cornelius in Acts 10:22); his actions break down powerful ethnic divisions. Many think that he, like Cornelius (Acts 10:1-2), believed in Israel's God but (because of Roman restrictions) had not been circumcised. But this may read too much into this text. As a person in authority himself he acknowledges Jesus' authority and honors him. He addresses Jesus as Lord (a respectful address). Twice he sends others to intercede with Jesus rather than going himself or having Jesus come into his house (on boundaries between Jews and Romans, see Acts 10:28). Though an authority and recognized as worthy by the elders, he expresses his own unworthiness compared to one who exemplifies another kind of authority. He speaks of Jesus' power to heal with only a word, a power he does not possess even with the power of Rome and its army behind him. In view of what Jesus hears, he commends the centurion's faith as unparalleled among the people of Israel.

This portrayal of a Gentile is an affirmation of God's good creation; it values human beings apart from their relation to Jesus. In telling the story, Luke's reference to another centurion in Acts 10:34-35 may well apply: "God shows no partiality, but in every nation anyone who fears him and does what is right is acceptable to him." Luke reminds us of many people outside the church, whose contributions to the good order and well-being of our communities are considerable. How often it is that such persons go unthanked by us, if not by God! Moreover, when such persons do enter the church, we so often think less highly of the gifts they bring with them than we ought.

The place of the Jews in the story is also important. A Jew/Gentile split is not acknowledged here. The Jewish elders, probably local synagogue leaders, are portrayed in kindly terms. They are trusted by the Roman officer, approach Jesus "earnestly" on his behalf, acknowledge Jesus as a healer, and accompany Jesus to his house. They are key mediators between Jesus and the Gentiles. This provides an occasion to think of comparable go-betweens in our own world who stand outside the church. Should we be listening more closely to the voices of other religious groups, for example, and what they might be saying about the kind of healing needed by the people with whom they have contact?

The faith of the centurion is not easy to define (see 5:20; 7:50; 8:25, 48; on a Gentile woman's faith, see Matt. 15:28). Jesus here makes a distinction among people who have faith, declaring that the centurion's faith is unmatched among Israelites (including the disciples!). Perhaps Jesus' comparative statement speaks to his confidence and trust in Jesus' authority only on the basis of what he had heard *about* Jesus. Unlike others who had come to faith, the centurion had never met Jesus and they have no direct contact here. Moreover, his belief that Jesus' word alone was powerful enough to heal was unlike that of others who had been able to associate Jesus' healings with his actual presence (see Jesus' claim in John 20:29 about those who have not seen and yet have come to believe).

Christians through the ages, mostly Gentiles (including Luke), have had a link to Jesus comparable to that of the centurion—only through words about him. We have believed because of what we have heard. This lifts up the great importance of what people hear us saying about Jesus. This text provides a moment to reflect on our public language about Jesus. How do people hear us? How does what we say come across to them? Might it be worth our trouble to find out, to listen more before we speak? Is our language so much oriented to the Christian scout troop that it is not understood by those out in the larger world? Does our language draw people toward Jesus or push them farther away? We might recognize here that what draws the centurion is the word about Jesus as a healer, a healer of more than spiritual ills—a much-neglected word about Jesus in mainstream Christianity. Note also that the one who is healed is not the one who has faith (as in 5:20). Those who have faith can be the mediators of the healing power of Jesus to others who may or may not have faith.

Third Sunday after Pentecost
Tenth Sunday in Ordinary Time/Proper 5

Lectionary	First Lesson	Psalm	Second Lesson	Gospel
Revised Common	1 Kgs. 17:17-24 or 17:8-16, (17-24)	Psalm 30 or 146	Gal. 1:11-24	Luke 7:11-17
Episcopal (BCP)	1 Kgs. 17:17-24	Psalm 30 or 30:1-6, 12-13	Gal. 1:11-24	Luke 7:11-17
Roman Catholic	1 Kgs. 17:17-24	Ps. 30:2, 4-6, 11-13	Gal. 1:11-19	Luke 7:11-17
Lutheran (LBW)	1 Kgs. 17:17-24	Psalm 30	Gal. 1:11-24	Luke 7:11-17

The texts for this Sunday hold several themes in common. First, they speak of the move from death to life. The parallel miracle stories in 1 Kings and Luke 7 both speak of this in literal terms, the raising of an only son of a widow from the dead; the Galatians text speaks of Paul's call. Second, the texts report that God is the one who has made this new life possible and speak of God as the one glorified. Third, they strike the note of public witness. Luke's story ends on a testimonial note that is parallel to that of the woman in Kings and is similar to that of Paul in Gal. 1:23-24.

Luke makes specific reference to 1 Kings 17, in 7:15 and in 4:25-26 (also, Luke 8:28 and 55 allude to 1 Kings 17:18 and 22; see the connections in last Sunday's texts). The links made to the prophetic stories in Kings rather than the classical prophets may be shaped by the common nature of the material (Paul is especially dependent upon Jeremiah). They are narratives about encounters with individuals in one kind of plight or another. This makes the healing activity of the prophets more prominent than is generally the case with Israel's prophets. The importance Luke gives to healing by the prophets and Jesus is extended in Acts to include Jesus' followers (see Acts 3:1-10; 4:30; 5:12-16), including raising from the dead (Peter in Acts 9:32-43).

More generally, the parallels between Jesus' ministry and the prophets are many: astute discernment of the human situation, concern for the poor and needy, ministry to Gentiles, healing, proclamation of both judgment and promise, reversal of popular expectations (a theme common to all three texts), and a future determined by whether one hears the prophet. Jesus is a prophet, yet more than a prophet (for instance, he will forgive sins; 7:48). One might also work from such a list to a consideration of the shape a prophetic ministry might take in our world (see also the listing below for Nathan in 2 Samuel 12).

FIRST LESSON: I KINGS 17:17-24

1 Kings 17–2 Kings 10 constitute a collection of stories about the prophets Elijah and Elisha. Generally, these stories are designed to serve several purposes: to resist the policies and practices of the evil rulers of Israel; to oppose the idolatrous worship of Baal (introduced into Israel's worship by king Ahab in 16:31-33); to enhance the role of the prophets in charting Israel through these dangerous times; and to magnify the God of Israel.

The stories in chapter 17 have been crafted from older legends to speak to each of these purposes. The opposition to Baal is sharply pronounced, especially the notion that Baal controlled life and death, whether in the human or natural order. The witness of these stories is that Israel's God is responsible, that matters of life and death are in God's hands. In each of the three stories God, through the word (vv. 4, 9, 16, 24), mediates life in and through various creatures: nonhumans, a poor widow, and the prophet himself. Regardless of the creatures' place in God's creation, God's effective word is at work through them to serve life.

In the first story (vv. 1-7), Israel's God is acclaimed as the Creator, who sees to the cycle of the dry and rainy seasons and who works through nonhuman creatures (ravens) to provide food and water to the faithful. This theme continues in chapter 18, where the conflict between Yahweh and Baal comes to a head. In the second story (vv. 8-16), Elijah is commanded to go to Zarephath, near the capital of Baal worship (Sidon, see 16:31), to demonstrate in the very center of the opposition that the God of Israel is in charge. God acts on behalf of the poor (those neglected by the political power structures) to provide food and works through even such lowly persons to care for the faithful. Here the prophet is dependent upon such a lowly one for his basic needs. Note also that Jesus appeals to this story in Luke 4:25-26 in a context that refers to opposition to his ministry, for which universal claims are made.

The third story (vv. 17-24; cf. the similar story of Elisha in 2 Kgs. 4:18-37) continues with the same characters in the same opposition-filled setting. This time the issue of life and death is more sharply raised. Israel's God is the God of life, not simply in the world of nature or in the provision of life-giving food and water, but even at the point where physical death has intruded upon human life. Wherever in all creation life and death issues are raised, there the God of Israel is shown to be the one who is the source of life. Here the prophet himself, like the ravens and the poor widow, is portrayed as the one who mediates the power of God for life by raising the widow's son from the dead.

The story begins with a report that the widow's son is no longer breathing. She accuses Elijah of deception with respect to his visit, that he has come to mediate the effects of her own sin—her son's death. This response to tragedy is as common today as then; this popular notion is reversed by the prophet's actions. Without defending himself, Elijah takes the son, lays him on his own bed (away from his mother), and prays to God, asking whether the widow is right in saying what she did about God. Elijah questions the common theology, and God's life-giving actions through him show this common theology to be bankrupt. Then he uses an existing healing ritual, which combines stretching his body over the boy (to communicate some of his own life to the boy) and a further prayer to God to restore his life (this time with an imperative). Note that prayer alone is not considered sufficient; Elijah combines prayer and a ritual that was thought to have healing effects (for a comparable combination, see 2 Kgs. 20:1-7). God responds to the prophet; in fact, God "listened" to Elijah! God does what Elijah wants done. The child's life returns, and he is restored. Elijah brings the boy back to his mother, speaking only the word the mother most wanted to hear: Your son is alive!

The mother's evaluation of the prophet is transformed. She speaks a confession that witnesses both to the power of the word of the Lord and to its mediation through the "man of God." In terms of agency, the activity of both prophet and God is considered crucial in the restoration process. The climactic note in the story lies not in the restoration as such but in the testimony of the woman (see 18:39). This witness sets the stage for the major confrontations of Elijah with the powers that be—both divine and human—in chapter 18. This prophet is "God's man" for this moment in a dangerous time for Israel and God's mission in the world.

Generally, then, the text has a dual movement that relates to the opposition to Baal. First, in its movement from death to life, the life-giving power of God is acclaimed. This is not basically about spiritual life; it is about physical life. God's healing work has to do with the whole person, not just one's spiritual life. In fact, God's work is about more than healing; it is about resurrection from the dead, from actual death to actual life.

Second, in its movement from the woman's accusation to her affirmation, a public witness is made to this God and God's prophet by a resident within Baal's own land. God and his effective witness have entered into enemy territory and have begun to conquer the powers of death *from within*—no military, political, or ecclesiastical activity here—through seemingly small gestures, feeble words, and the witness of a lowly woman. One small healing act here and there, and more testifying women like her, and the word about this life-giving God will get around!

SECOND LESSON: GALATIANS 1:11-24

Continuing from last Sunday, Paul engages in further defense of his apostolicity. He has been called, not through other humans, but through a direct revelation from Christ. This gospel that he preaches is of divine origin. The gospel has been delivered to him by God; it is not the product of his own mind or that of another.

In this segment, Paul is dependent upon Jeremiah, not least because Jeremiah is called to be "a prophet to the nations" (Jer. 1:5). He understands himself, like Jeremiah (Jer. 1:5), to be called from the womb (v. 15). Moreover, his defense against those with another gospel reflects Jeremiah's conflict with the false prophets (see Jeremiah 23; 28), who speak visions of their own fancy, not the words of the Lord (23:16; 14:14).

Paul proceeds to tell his own story—the Damascus road experience and subsequent events in his early life in the church (see Acts 9:1-22; 22:4-16; 26:9-18). Note that, however important his story is, Paul does not use conversion language to describe what happened. He centers on God's *revelation* to him (vv. 12, 16), and his call to "proclaim" Christ to the Gentiles. Paul presents this as a call to vocation; he does not, however, consider his call to be paradigmatic for other Christians (God calls people in various ways). The call itself does not center this text; instead, his call revealed to him where the emphasis is to be placed: the proclamation of the gospel to the Gentiles. He has a message from God to proclaim, not his own experience. Any recollection of personal experience should be for the purpose of glorifying God, not the one who has had the experience (v. 24). The reason Paul retells this story is to ground his call in God's revelation rather than in what he has (not) been in the past, what he has thought or accomplished, or contacts he has had with other church leaders.

In an unusual move, at least for many, Paul rehearses his life without reference to feelings of guilt over his persecution of the church and his zeal for the Jewish traditions (as in Phil. 3:4-11). Paul is not driven by guilt to proclaim the message of Christ. He is driven by God's call, and his past remains truly past, not something that should continue to burden him. At the same time, his reference to being called from the womb and graciously set apart then suggests that his experience in Judaism, and his zeal for the ancestral traditions, were not without value for the call that he now receives. Paul does not believe he has to denigrate his past in order to be caught up in this new reality. Indeed, the abilities and strengths that he exhibited in his earlier life are gifts of God the Creator and God can now make good use of them to another end. Those of us in the church need to find better ways of honoring who people were before they became Christians and recognizing God's work among them during that time as having

THIRD SUNDAY AFTER PENTECOST/PROPER 5

continuing value for the new life to which they have been called. Our much-too-easy language about killing and making alive all too often denigrates this creative work of God in people.

Paul's rehearsal of his early itinerary serves to distance him from other church leaders. Paul's initial time after his call is spent in reflection and meditation in the Arabian peninsula. This experience continues to focus on the relationship with God and further grounds his call from God. When he does go to Jerusalem to meet with key officials, it is clear that what he preaches has already come from God and not from other human beings ("flesh and blood"), even from important church leaders. His contact with them had to do with introducing himself and developing a strategy for his mission work. Paul thus combines well an independence with respect to his calling and an interdependence with other people of faith in working together to further the work of the Gospel.

GOSPEL: LUKE 7:11-17

Only Luke includes this narrative, but it follows the typical structure of a miracle story: setting, predicament, encounter with Jesus, miraculous effect, and response of wonder. Luke tells two other stories about dead persons being resuscitated, by Jesus—of another only child (8:40-56)—and by Peter—of a female disciple (Acts 9:36-43). The latter makes clear that such miracles were not unique to Jesus, in the New Testament as well as the Old.

As in last Sunday's text from Luke, the identification of Jesus as prophet commands attention (see at 7:1-10). The parallels with the story of Elijah's raising of the widow's son in 1 Kings 17:17-24 are especially noteworthy, including verbal details (see the introduction to this Sunday's texts). The emphasis in Kings on God's power to move people from death to life is also emphasized here, as is the reversal of popular expectations (a common Lukan theme; cf. Mary's song in 1:52-53). Luke uses the Kings text only indirectly; the point would not be to speak of fulfillment, but to show that Jesus' own ministry clearly stands in the prophetic line. The following text (7:18-35) sorts out the relationship between Jesus and John the Baptist; one purpose is to show that, while John's prophetic role is deeply significant, Jesus is the prophet par excellence (note the link back to this text in 7:22). While Jesus surpasses the prophets, Luke's identification of him as a prophet is an important statement as to Jesus' identity. The references to a prophet in this chapter and elsewhere should also be linked with Acts 3:22-23, where Jesus is identified with the prophet like Moses whom God will raise up (Deut. 18:15-18).

Jesus' journey across Galilee takes him to Nain (near Nazareth), where he encounters a funeral procession. An only son of a widow has died and was about to be buried, leaving the widow without support. Jesus' compassion (Luke first identifies Jesus as Lord here), a profound suffering-with, prompts four actions on his part: He speaks tenderly to the mother, touches the stretcher (a crossing of purity lines, see Num. 5:1-4; 19:16), commands the young man to rise (the healing occurs by Jesus' word alone, cf. 7:7), and, after he sits up and speaks, gives him to his mother. Note that Jesus' concern for the mother pervades the story and brackets the encounter. The emphasis placed on Jesus' teachings and miracles tends to neglect the "pastoral care" that Jesus displays at such moments. The tenderness and gentleness of Jesus, which can be over-sentimentalized, is an integral part of the Gospel witness (and may qualify the typical understanding of prophet). This testimony is also part of Luke's effort to answer the question, Who is Jesus?

The story concludes with the response of those who had observed Jesus' action and a report of those who later heard about it. Such a conclusion suggests that the spreading of the word about Jesus is even more important than the miracle itself. Jesus is not simply a miracle worker, but is to be identified in more comprehensive terms (Luke already identifies Jesus as Savior in 2:11). But it may be that the hearers need to be "hooked" by one or another story about Jesus before they can be led more fully and deeply into who Jesus is and what he is about.

The people were afraid; earlier in Luke this language is used in response to divine action or visitation (1:11-13; 2:9-10). This healing is a witness to the presence of God. Remarkably, the people glorify *God*, not Jesus, and speak of the raising as an effect of a favorable visitation by God; they understand that Jesus is not working alone, but that God's presence and activity in and through him is the decisive factor. Jesus himself is acknowledged as a great prophet whom God has raised up (the verb is passive, and may anticipate Jesus' resurrection). This acclaim regarding Jesus spreads like wildfire throughout the country, including Judea.

Fourth Sunday after Pentecost
Eleventh Sunday in Ordinary Time/Proper 6

Lectionary	First Lesson	Psalm	Second Lesson	Gospel
Revised Common	2 Sam. 11:26—12:10, 13-15 or 1 Kgs. 21:1-10, (11-14), 15-21a	Psalm 32 or 5:1-8	Gal. 2:15-21	Luke 7:36—8:3
Episcopal (BCP)	2 Sam. 11:26—12:10, 13-15	Psalm 32 or 32:1-8	Gal. 2:11-21	Luke 7:36-50
Roman Catholic	2 Sam. 12:7-10, 13	Ps. 32:1-2, 5, 7, 11	Gal. 2:16, 19-21	Luke 7:36—8:3 or 7:36-50
Lutheran (LBW)	2 Sam. 11:26—12:10, 13-15	Psalm 32	Gal. 2:11-21	Luke 7:36-50

Ma Bell urges us to reach out and touch someone. She says more than she knows: male–female relationships are often such that the only safe way to touch anymore is over the phone. Many women know that being touched by men has led to abuse, and one can understand if they are on the alert. Many men are wary of touching women, lest their intentions be misunderstood. Most of us have good intuitions as to appropriate boundaries and differing comfort zones. Yet, in this time of renegotiation regarding appropriate roles, numerous grey areas often leave us baffled and uncomfortable. One danger is that we will cover over this reality, and let things go on as if everything is alright or in time will pass away like a bad dream. But that is a formula for failure. We need to talk about these issues of male–female relationships as openly as possible.

The passages from Samuel and Luke could provide an occasion for doing so. Though the theme of boundaries is probably not what has brought these texts together, it is a reality in both texts. David violates these boundaries with Bathsheba. Jesus' relationship with the woman who is a sinner is exemplary, though the issue of boundaries is sharply raised by those who observe his behavior with her (7:39) and may well be raised by many a modern reader. This conflict over the law could also draw in the text from Galatians.

These texts once again have in common the role of the prophet. Nathan's role with David issues in a sharp condemnation of David's behavior. The role of Jesus as prophet is a theme that Luke has been exploring. Yet, Jesus' behavior with the woman brings his identity as a prophet under suspicion. While the prophetic role of judgment is drawn in both texts, more sharply delineated is the role of the prophet as one who forgives sin.

FIRST LESSON: 2 SAMUEL 11:26—12:15

This text and the alternate (1 Kings 21) have to do with the confrontation of a king (David, Ahab) by a prophet (Nathan, Elijah) regarding an issue of justice (the taking of Uriah's wife and the taking of Naboth's vineyard) about which God is highly displeased.

David's affair with Bathsheba, followed by Nathan's "You are the man!" speech, has long fascinated interpreters. The narrative themes of Joshua-Kings regarding the people of Israel are here played out in the life of an individual—sin, prophetic indictment, repentance, judgment, and forgiveness. David embodies Israel in his own life. Personal story and public story are here integrated. This story is part of the Succession Narrative (2 Samuel 9–20; 1 Kings 1–2) with its question, Who will succeed David as king of Israel? The answer is given in 12:24 (Solomon). A public affair provides the context for a private affair.

Readers are invited to explore the complex relationship of David's personal life and the public order. The sins of David—here centered in male–female relationships—have public effects, especially given his role as king. Generally, what individuals do counts; their words and deeds make a difference beyond their own lives and have deep effects on their public world. In this case, David's violation of boundaries with Bathsheba, the wife of Uriah, has significant effects upon the good order of Israelite society.

Our text is introduced by a description of David's adultery and Uriah's murder (11:2-25). David is the one with power; it has just been demonstrated with the Ammonites (11:1). All that power is now suddenly focused on a single individual, a "very beautiful" woman named Bathsheba (11:2). David doesn't turn his eyes upon seeing her bathing; rather, she becomes his prey, the object of his sexual desire. It doesn't matter that she is a married woman or that he is a married man; it doesn't matter that her father and her husband have participated in David's military successes; it doesn't matter what she might think about having sex with him; it doesn't matter that the sharp imbalance in power between them leaves her without choice. Boundaries do not matter. David wants to have sex with her, sex without love. In the face of such a combination of power and desire, Bathsheba can only acquiesce. What David wants, David gets. Right away. The narrative conveys this point by its spare comment: David sent his servants "to get her, and she came to him, and he lay with her" (11:4). Bathsheba is given no voice, no introductory courtesies, no time to consider the matter, no out. Right to the king's bedroom. The king will have his way with her on his schedule and on his turf. Today we would call David a rapist.

This violation of Bathsheba leads David into a litany of lies in an effort to cover his tracks. Such deception eventually leads to Uriah's death.

While Bathsheba mourns, David plans to move her into his harem. And, once again, the spare comment of 11:26-27 shows that she remains without voice or power in this Davidic move. But God is not without moves to make or power to exercise. Into this moment God sends a prophet. The role of Nathan in confronting David is crucial. Observing Nathan's actions, we may delineate the following prophetic tasks; with the Lukan text in mind one could also track how Jesus fulfills these prophetic roles.

1. *Vigilance and discernment*—Nathan is alert regarding developing situations and discerns what kind of word from God is needed, for the sake of both individual and community.

2. *Wisdom*—Nathan is wise in his choice of the literary vehicle for the word he has to bring. It is a judgment-eliciting parable, told for the purpose of drawing a response from David that would carry its own judgment. The parable works because David's suspicions are not raised and yet David could not escape the force of it when Nathan gives the clue. The parable also works because it increases David's emotional involvement and it raises obvious justice issues, focused on the use of oppressive power. It connects with David's own commitments to justice.

3. *Boldness and clarity*—Nathan confronts the king with a critical word, in such a way that repentance is invited, and he is clear regarding God's perspective: David's deed is displeasing to God (cited four times). Nathan focuses on David's relationship with God, recalling God's gracious acts on his behalf as the basis for the accusation rather than the law (vv. 7-8). God has given him so much! This is a rebellion against grace more than the law.

4. *Words of judgment*—These words correlate with the nature of the sin. The punishment fits the crime (vv. 10-12), a word that is later fulfilled (2 Sam. 13:18; 16:22; 1 Kings 2). David has taken away and so something comparable will be taken from him. Sharp questions about God are raised here that are not easily resolved. God's judgment makes things worse. Instead of one murder and one adultery/rape, there are many of each. Yet, this may make the text say more than it actually does. The text is a statement about the moral order, which God facilitates. But God does not introduce these effects; they grow out of the deed itself and royal sins have great effects. The God linkage, however, makes clear to David that his sin has these effects and God is the one with whom he finally has to do and not some impersonally functioning moral order. The language of v. 15b is harsh and unusual for God's action (here of illness) toward an individual; it may best be understood as a sharp statement of divine maintenance of the moral order.

5. *Word of forgiveness*—Nathan responds to David's repentance with a word of forgiveness. No reference is made to the law or to sacrifice. The

word is effective in its being spoken. This word works against the effects of the sin, so that the future will be less of a disaster. At least David does not die (see Lev. 20:10), but the effects announced in vv. 10-12 seem not to be ameliorated at all, although Solomon is born (v. 24).

This text may be used to point up human sinfulness and its snowballing effects beyond the sinner. But the specific sins ought not be ignored and the root sin ought not be narrowed to adultery, as if these were consenting adults and Bathsheba becomes as guilty as David (Nathan does not confront Bathsheba). The nature of the sin involved as I have sketched it out above needs forthright discussion. This text also shows the importance of human repentance and the positive effects that that can have for the life of the community. Above all, the text witnesses to God: sending a prophet with a word of both justice and forgiveness. The sequel shows that God also begins again, showering love on the child of an illicit union and working to shape a more positive future.

SECOND LESSON: GALATIANS 2:11-21

Paul speaks of a conflict over the place of the law in the Christian's life. This conflict was generated by a significant change in the life of the early church—the spread of Christianity to Gentiles. This issue had been debated at a council in Jerusalem (Acts 15) but had not been finally resolved. In connection with a visit of Peter to Antioch, Paul minces no words in condemning him for his compromised stance on the matter of law observance. Peter had gotten it right initially in setting aside food laws and eating freely with Gentiles. But in the face of an evaluative visit from the Jerusalem "national offices," he had backed off from such a practice and persuaded other Jews (including Barnabas) to do the same. Paul interprets Peter's actions as more than a matter of expediency, though they are that. The "truth of the Gospel" is at stake in such actions and his "selective freedom" has negative implications for reaching out to the Gentile world. Paul uses this story as a launching point for the verses that follow.

At the same time, the law does not cease to be important for Paul (see also 3:19-25). The issue that Paul confronts has to do with how the law is to function for Christians. While Paul is interested in particular laws such as those regarding food (v. 12) and circumcision (see 5:1-4; 6:12-13), he focuses on a larger issue. He is concerned to address the claim by some that observance of the law of Moses is necessary for salvation. Christians are brought into a right relationship with God, not by obeying the law, but "through faith in Jesus Christ." Yet, in addressing this issue, Paul stresses the importance of law. It was through the law (that is, in its revealing of sin, through which we are "found to be sinners") that he "died to the law" as a way of salvation (2:19). The law drove him to Christ; through faith in Christ, who loved him and gave himself up for him, he has been justified.

The oft-memorized v. 20 is worthy of special attention. It is clear from the phrase, "insofar as I live in the flesh," that Paul does in fact continue to live. It is not simply Christ who lives in Paul, as if Paul's person had been displaced by Christ. Rather, the old Adam has died, has been crucified with Christ; now Paul lives as one whose new life has been received from Christ, dependent for his life on "the Son of God who has loved me and given himself up for me." Without Christ he would be dead in his sins. Nothing that Paul has done has enabled him to claim this new life; so Paul's "I" is not able to stand alone. In the language of Col. 3:3: "For you have died, and your life is hidden with Christ in God."

Christians may find it comforting to observe that the early church had its conflicts too, not least conflicts over the law. Christians claim, following Paul, that we are freed from the law as a means to salvation, but at the same time we realize that we have not been freed from conflicts about the law that our continuing sins generate. What we have not as commonly seen is that these conflicts about the law may bend back and compromise our claims about the gospel. For example: if you would be a Christian then you must obey this law or that law; or, you are not truly a Christian unless you do so. In subtle, and not so subtle, ways the church has built behavioral conditions into its gospel message. And whenever it has done so, that message has become "another gospel." Many churchly conflicts about the law focus on a particular biblical law or "way of doing things in the church" and the issue of their continuing applicability for Christian faith and life. These issues become particularly pressing in times of change. The end of the twentieth century has seen massive societal changes that deeply impinge upon our churchly life. In such times, holding on to certain laws or ways and insisting they are integral to being a Christian is a constant temptation. In this conversation, we have not done very well in learning from past experience, such as reflected in this text. One is given to wonder whether we clearly see that in our conflicts over the observance of one law or another we see the implications for our understanding of the gospel.

GOSPEL: LUKE 7:36—8:3

This text (unique to Luke) has several unusual elements, not least those involving women: Jesus' relationship with the female "sinner" and the list of women disciples and supporters. The high role given to women testifies to their important place in the early Christian movement.

The story is set in the house of a Pharisee named Simon who, for unknown reasons, had asked Jesus to eat with him. Jesus eats with tax collectors, sinners, *and* Pharisees (see 7:34)! Tension is created when a woman from the street enters and, with Jesus reclining at table, begins to kiss his feet and anoint them with expensive oils. Her actions are commonly interpreted as a sign of hospitality (and distinguished from the anointing for burial story, for instance, Mark 14:3-9), an ironic assumption of the role of host; but her weeping, the only voice she is given in the story, shows that more is at stake for her. Why is she weeping? Lament, grief, contrition, and gratitude come to mind, but the logic of the riddle Jesus tells suggests gratitude (= love). She loves much because she has been forgiven much; this suggests that she has been forgiven by Jesus on an occasion prior to the dinner (as v. 47 says; see NRSV; NEB). Hence, Jesus' contrast of her actions and Simon's (vv. 44-46) have to do with a hospitality that is rooted in gratitude.

Simon thinks (not says) that Jesus is not a true prophet for he allows this "kind of woman" to touch him (a concern for purity in relating to the unclean, another boundary issue; see Lev. 5:1-5). He assumes he knows who a prophet is and the place this woman has in the order of things; ironically, Jesus is a prophet and knows really what "kind of woman" this is. Jesus, having read his mind, puts a story to him like the one Nathan told to David—a judgment-eliciting riddle. Simon, in saying that the person who was forgiven the greater debt would be more grateful, implicitly acknowledges "what kind of woman" this really is. He is less grateful because, unlike the woman, he has not recognized the depths of his own sinfulness and his need for forgiveness. Jesus then assures her of her forgiveness, and announces that her response of faith and Jesus' word of forgiveness entails her salvation.

The question raised by the dinner guests regarding Jesus' identity in view of his word of forgiveness is a question addressed to the reader (v. 49). This act stands in the prophetic tradition, as Nathan's word of God's forgiveness to David shows (2 Sam. 12:13), but Jesus as the one who forgives raises the issue of whether he is not more than a prophet (see 5:24). Jesus tells the woman to go in peace. But to what community does she go? Perhaps to the community noted in 8:1-3, but the reader also needs to answer this question.

This text from Luke is only partially helpful in dealing with boundary issues. In at least one sense we ought to be disturbed at what the text does not say. If the woman is a prostitute, as many exegetes think (compare v. 39 and v. 34 with Matt. 21:31-32), then she is a victim of abusive behavior. It no doubt was as true then as it is today: 80–85 percent of prostitutes have been sexually abused during their growing-up years by someone they knew. The so-called victimless crime of prostitution is filled with victims, who often come to believe they deserve their lot in life and continue to submit to victimization. Today we must recognize what the text does not: this woman is a victim of abuse and we should pronounce a sharp word of judgment on those who have made her so, and on the church, whose voice is strangely muted on this matter.

One motif in the Gospels that might be helpful is the role that touching plays in Jesus' ministry. Jesus reaches out and touches other people, both men and women, particularly those who are in need of healing. Many people also reach out to touch Jesus and Jesus responds to their touching in nonerotic ways. These texts should make it possible to talk about touching in ways that commend appropriate modes of relationship. In Luke, the touching between Jesus and this sister of the street is as scandalous today as it was in the first century. Certainly Jesus cannot be a man of God, or he would not have permitted this sister to touch him so. He would certainly have been more protective of his reputation. He would certainly have known from the law that issues of a life of purity would be raised. When we hear Jesus say, "from the time I came in she has not ceased to kiss my feet," we may wonder whether Jesus was not letting the situation get out of hand. Simon and the other gawkers no doubt interpret all this in erotic ways. They look at what goes on in order to label it, and that is all they want to know and say. But Jesus doesn't play it safe; he makes himself vulnerable in the presence of the religious authorities. He will not be put off, and he lets her touching go on and on.

It seems clear that the woman sensed something in Jesus that she had not sensed in other men with whom she often had to do. She sensed that she did not have to be afraid, that she could reach out and touch him, indeed kiss him profusely, and not have to worry about what he might do, or that he might misinterpret her actions. In turn, her loving, touching acts of gratitude and devotion are approved by Jesus: she acts in this way, he says, because she has been forgiven. Jesus proclaims that forgiveness publicly both for her sake and for all the others to see.

Our sins may not be as socially obvious as those of our sister in this text, but the depths of our own mistreatment of one another are such that we have not one stone to throw. But we, too, have heard the public word of Jesus: you are forgiven. Yet, that is not the end of the matter for us. There are other words to speak and deeds to be done. The gratitude shown by this sister of the street provides a pattern for our response to the God who has forgiven us. But there is more. Jesus also washed feet, and he instructed his disciples to follow his example. That will entail both washing and being washed. The way in which Jesus responds to the washing and the touching of our sister provides a clue for our responding to one another. We know the healing that can come from the gentle touching of others. By exhibiting our love in this and other ways, we can show forth that we are indeed forgiven ones.

That will not be easy or risk-free, but let the way in which Jesus responds to the loving touch of a forgiven one guide us in our relationships with one another as male and female. So, when a person of the opposite sex comes up to you or me, they will be able to sense that they are in the presence of a friend. And they will be able to reach out to us, perhaps even touch us, knowing that we will respond in such a way that they need not be afraid.

Fifth Sunday after Pentecost
Twelfth Sunday in Ordinary Time/Proper 7

Lectionary	First Lesson	Psalm	Second Lesson	Gospel
Revised Common	Isa. 65:1-9 or 1 Kgs. 19:1-4, (5-7), 8-15a	Ps. 22:19-28 or Psalm 42 and 43	Gal. 3:23-29	Luke 8:26-39
Episcopal (BCP)	Zech. 12:8-10; 13:1	Ps. 63:1-8	Gal. 3:23-29	Luke 9:18-24
Roman Catholic	Zech. 12:10-11; 13:1	Ps. 63:2-6, 8-9	Gal. 3:26-29	Luke 9:18-24
Lutheran (LBW)	Zech. 12:7-10	Ps. 63:1-8	Gal. 3:23-29	Luke 9:18-24

The connection between Galatians and Luke lifts up the freedom of those who have been saved, the freedom to be what they were created to be, whether Jew or Gentile, slave or free, male or female. Jesus Christ has the authority to make even the most possessed of people, even those who seem to be beyond saving, even those whose lives are consumed by evil, free from the powers that enslave them. The powers of evil and those who embody that evil will not finally prevail; Isaiah speaks of their judgment, the salvation of the righteous remnant, and the creation of a new heaven and earth—the kingdom of God that has come near in Jesus.

FIRST LESSON: ISAIAH 65:1-9

This text comes from that part of Isaiah often called Third Isaiah (56–66). These texts are addressed to Israelites that have returned from Babylonian exile but encountered in Canaan something less than the glorious future announced by Second Isaiah. The dispirited people respond in several ways to these hardships; some return to idolatrous ways while others remain faithful. The latter often have to contend with persecution from the former (see 66:5), though the divisions within the community are not always so clear. The message of this prophet varies, depending upon which of these audiences he has most in mind. The word of judgment is addressed to the idolaters primarily, but may also function as a warning to those who might be tempted to such practices, or even as a word of promise that the enemies of the righteous will finally be defeated (the rhythm of judgment and salvation oracles pertains throughout these chapters, including the text from Isaiah 66 in two weeks).

Isaiah 65 is God's response to the questions asked in 64:12 (the people speak from 63:15 through 64:12) regarding why God has been silent and has not delivered the people from their hardships. Chapter 65 is God's defense of divine actions in the face of the questions; it is a pathos-filled oracle that mixes indictment and announcements of judgment and salvation. The pathos of God is especially evident in vv. 1-2. God was ready to listen, but the people did not speak. God says, "I held out my hands all day long" (a gesture of prayer), but the prayers were not returned. The people followed their own will (devices) rather than God's. They walked in ways that were evil, not good. It is remarkable to hear God saying, "Here I am, here I am," to make sure that the people know their prayers were welcome and that God was available to hear them, "all day long." To think out loud with people about the kind of God that is portrayed here could prove interesting.

What kind of God would speak in such a way to people? This is not a distant, aloof God. This God is affected by what people do (or don't do). What might it mean to speak of a God who reacts to what is going on in the world, who is truly so responsive and so affected? This is not the immutable (unchanging) God of whom some theologians speak. The people's nonresponse has generated in God a response that would otherwise not have been. Note the language: this is "a people who *provoke me* to my face" (v. 3a). Indeed, this language of God has a certain emotional intensity (read vv. 1-3a out loud). What does it mean to speak of God as one who has emotions? This language is anthropomorphic, of course, but so is virtually all language about God; it is no less anthropomorphic to speak of God as one who thinks and speaks. Perhaps we hesitate to use such language for God because we trust emotions less than we do intellect. Or, perhaps a male image for God gets in the way ("Big boys don't cry!")? We consider human beings who do not show emotion as being less than healthy. Our God is a healthy God!

What kind of relationship must this God have with people to speak like this? This is not a God who couldn't care less about what the people do. This God is hurt (!) by the lack of response on the part of the human party to the relationship. What does it mean to have a God who gets so caught up in relationships? This God is committed to the relationship with the people and is genuinely concerned when things do not go well. To have people hear about a God who is so affected by what they do could prompt repentance or enable them to recognize the kind of God with whom they have to do.

The problem was not with God but with the people, who did not speak and were rebellious, walking "in a way that is not good" (v. 2), especially in the area of worship. The people are involved in various idolatrous and pagan rituals; they offer sacrifices that burn in God's nostrils rather than have a pleasing odor. And these people claim a holiness, a closeness to God, that excludes other people from worship rather than welcomes them.

To this kind of worship God will respond; God will not keep silent. But the word God speaks is not one for which the people yearn to hear (64:12); it is a word of judgment. Note the language used for judgment: God will visit the people's iniquities back upon their own head. God does not introduce something new into the situation. God will visit *their own* iniquities upon them, measuring a response that is correspondent to their own deeds. They will reap what they have sown; what goes around comes around.

Yet, God makes a distinction among the *chosen* people, between "my people who have sought me" and "you who forsake the Lord" (vv. 10-11). This distinction is laid out in specific terms in vv. 13-15 ("my servants . . . but you")—judgment for the wicked and blessing for the faithful remnant. This word of blessing for God's servants begins in vv. 8-9; good wine can be found in the cluster of grapes that is Israel, and God will bless the remnant from the Northern Kingdom (Jacob) and Southern Kingdom (Judah) on the land. This word of salvation for the faithful comes to a climax in the description of the new heaven and the new earth in 65:17-25.

SECOND LESSON: GALATIANS 3:23-29

In this text Paul speaks further of the relationship of law and faith. Until we had come to faith in Christ, the law served to guard us along life's way, much like a slave who escorts a child to and from school. Paul also uses the language of imprisonment for the law, as that which restricts and confines rather than opens life up to freedom in the gospel. But now that faith in Christ shapes our life, the law no longer functions in the same way. The law does not cease to have value; it still serves to protect life in the world, even promote such life. But faith rather than the law brings people to Christ. We do not need to measure ourselves over against the law to discern whether we are right with God, or use the law to take our "spiritual temperature" to make sure we are still a Christian, or to preserve that relationship.

In and through baptism we have put on Christ; Christ has become our clothing. This implies no loss of our identity as human beings, but because we are clothed with Christ we are enabled to stand before God justified (see 2:20 in last week's text). And because we are now in Christ, the descendant of Abraham (3:16), we are reckoned as heirs of the promise given to Abraham (see 4:7); we are "the Israel of God" (6:16), full-fledged children of Abraham. This is our identity, who we have become in the deepest nooks and crannies of our being. This is not a disguise or temporary status or surface identification. This identity is as real as if we were a direct descendant of Abraham. We no longer have to think about words or deeds by which we can become such children or maintain such a status; by faith this is who we are.

This oneness in Christ means that all divisions into which human beings are commonly divided—race, status, and gender are noted—are of no account in relating to God (see Rom. 10:12; 1 Cor. 12:13; Col. 3:11). These divisions are life situations into which people are born, rather than become later in life (at least in that culture). We are implicitly invited to think of other divisions "by birth" that are (or may become) a dividing reality among us—biological, sexual, racial, ethnic, social, economic, religious—and to ask whether we are promoting these distinctions in ways that are inimical to the gospel. Are certain individuals or groups of people being made second-class citizens in your congregation in any way? How welcoming is your congregation to all types of folk, whether in worship or leadership roles or general conversation? Paul is not trying to eradicate the differences that do exist among people, say, between male and female. In fact, such differences are a gift to both church and society. Rather, Paul here makes strong claims regarding the unity of the church, a unity that is grounded in only one thing: the gospel of Jesus Christ.

Religious convictions and practices—"how we do things in our church"—have often contributed to and reinforced such divisions; circumcision is one such example, a practice that perpetuated divisions between Jew and Gentile and between male and female. Baptism does not create such divisions; it is an inclusive sacrament that welcomes and incorporates all without distinction into the body of Christ. Recent efforts to ground the abolition of slavery and the ordination of women in this and related texts are being true to Paul's convictions, though Paul did not carry his own thinking this far (see 1 Cor. 14:34-35). Every person, regardless of station in life, is at home in the church and is to feel equally welcome there; no one is a second-class citizen. A diversity of functions is indeed called for (see 1 Cor. 12:12-31), but that diversity is in service of the one body.

GOSPEL: LUKE 8:26-39

This text has parallels in both Matthew (8:28-34) and Mark (5:1-20). While their identity is uncertain (see the NRSV footnote to v. 26), both Gerasa and Gadara were Gentile cities (the only such locale for Jesus' ministry in Luke)—note the presence of swine, unclean animals for Jews. Luke has Jesus confront unclean spirits before (4:31-37, 41; 8:2) and after (9:37-43; 11:14-28) this occasion. Jesus also gives exorcising power to his disciples (9:1; 10:17-20; cf. Acts 16:16-39; 19:11-20). Yet, even those who are not among the core followers of Jesus have this power (9:49-50), as do Jews (11:19) and others in that world (belief in demons is widespread).

The temptation of Jesus by the devil (4:1-13) sets the groundwork for these confrontations. The temptation establishes that the powers of evil are a reality in the world which Jesus confronts; they are transpersonal, cosmic powers that have become established in God's world (the Gospels do not speculate on their origin). They are anti-God forces who oppose the will of God for peace, wholeness, and salvation; they are not irresistible, but can gain access to people's individual and corporate lives and control them, with deeply damaging physical, mental, or spiritual effects (to reduce demon-possession to mental illness limits the range of the Gospels' witness to the power of evil). We today may not often use demon language, but evil is no less real for that. In fact, the absence of a common language for this reality may lull us into thinking that evil is not so pervasive and that we are the ones in control. The powers of evil have deeply dominating effects in the lives of individuals, and have become "institutionalized" in our corporate structures; they can even get "inside" the church. Now and again, stark manifestations of the controlling power of evil appear on our screens (Bosnia, Rwanda, the latest "tragedy" in our neighborhood) and we are given a fearful glimpse of forces beyond our control. At such times our comfort levels are diminished, and we may even recognize that such powers lurk very close to our own hearts and homes. And we may see our desperate need for one who, by the finger of God, can resist the tempter and cast out demons.

These evil powers know Jesus' proper identity (4:3, 9) and they rightly perceive that he is a threat to their influence in the world and control of people. Luke establishes at the beginning of the Gospel (4:1-13) that, through the use of the word of God, Jesus can resist their powers. Though Jesus does not finally eliminate them or their sphere of influence at this point (see 4:13), Satan's "fall" is already underway (10:18). These evil powers will appear as a challenge to Jesus' mission in a variety of forms in Luke—in confrontations by possessed people or in more subtle betrayals (Judas in 22:3). Questions about Jesus' authority and power over evil will be raised along the way (4:36; 11:14-23). This Sunday's text is the most detailed and bizarre of such stories; perhaps the destructiveness of the demons is related to Gentile territory, anticipating opposition to the Gentile mission while establishing that Jesus' power over even the worst that evil can wage knows no boundaries. In this text, a specific individual and his deep-seated problems becomes the focus for Jesus' compassion and healing.

This story follows a common structure for exorcisms (see 4:31-37). It begins with a confrontation of Jesus by a demon-possessed person. The range and debilitating nature of the man's disorders—he could not be fully restrained by others—is related to the "many demons" that had entered him. Next, the man—actually the demons that possess him—correctly identifies Jesus (with the name given Mary by the angel, 1:32!) and loudly engages him. That the demons know the identity of Jesus may indicate supernatural knowledge (see 4:41), and may be an ironic way of highlighting the lack of such knowledge on the part of many (see 4:22; 9:9, 18-19). While knowing the name is sometimes thought to provide power over the named, that is shown here not always to be the case. Those who name the name of Jesus (and the name of God as well)—even the demons—do not control the one named. But Jesus' ability to gain the name of the devil that plagues the man (or us), to name the problem, also entails the power to overcome it.

The detail of the ensuing dialogue and description is unusual. Jesus' command to the unclean spirit to come out of the man had not finally been effective (v. 29a) and the conversation continues. The exchange of names is striking; the name Legion (a company of some five thousand soldiers) is as descriptive of the man's situation as is the name he gives Jesus. The demons recognize that Jesus is in full control of the situation (vv. 31-32) and beg not to be sent to the abyss (the underworld, where evil spirits are imprisoned; 2 Pet. 2:4) but into the swine (ironically, for the unclean ask to enter into the unclean). Perhaps they think they can escape, but it proves to be only a self-chosen means of annihilation. Though strange and destructive, Jesus puts their request into effect. That the possessed swine rush to drown themselves is not due to Jesus' directive, but is testimony to the destructive powers of evil. Sensitivity to effects upon the animal world and to the economic support of the swineherders is here set aside (Jewish readers would have viewed the destruction of unclean animals positively). The point stressed is Jesus' authority over the powers of evil. To rid the world of evil and to restore peace and wholeness will often disrupt the normal course of life.

The effect of the exorcism is more extended than usual. When the people hear the news and confirm for themselves that the man has been healed, their response is fear (vv. 35, 37) and they successfully ask Jesus to leave the area. Perhaps the fear is due to the disruption of their normal lives and—in a more focused way—to the challenge to their easy identification of where the power of evil was to be located in their midst (in the bizarre, the tombs, and the wilds). Perhaps the fear is simply a deep sense that God has been at work among them (see 7:16), and God is not as easily managed. The angels' word to the shepherds at Jesus' birth (2:10, "do not be afraid") is a word about this Jesus that these people desperately need to hear.

Hence, once again, the import of the mission to the Gentiles; "the harvest is plentiful" (10:2).

The man who had been healed has the opposite reaction. He sits at the feet of Jesus (cf. Mary in 10:39), a new man. While he is not allowed to join Jesus' immediate followers, he obeys Jesus' command and spreads abroad all that God has done for him. The close connection made between healing and witness is a paradigm for all who have experienced the power of God in their lives. Remarkably, Jesus chooses to be dependent on such voices of gratitude for getting the word out. What the healed one says makes a difference regarding the shape the future of the mission takes (in this case, among the Gentiles). Interestingly, Jesus sends him away to speak about *God's* action in his life, not to what Jesus has done. But the narrator speaks of the man spreading a word about Jesus. This is not a disobedient act. The narrator thereby speaks of God acting through Jesus; in him the kingdom of God has come near (see 11:20).

Sixth Sunday after Pentecost
Thirteenth Sunday in Ordinary Time/Proper 8

Lectionary	First Lesson	Psalm	Second Lesson	Gospel
Revised Common	1 Kgs. 19:15-16, 19-21 or 2 Kgs. 2:1-2, 6-14	Psalm 16 or 77:1-2, 11-20	Gal. 5:1, 13-25	Luke 9:51-62
Episcopal (BCP)	1 Kgs. 19:15-16, 19-21	Psalm 16 or 16:5-11	Gal. 5:1, 13-25	Luke 9:51-62
Roman Catholic	1 Kgs. 19:16b, 19-21	Ps. 16: 1-2, 5, 7-11	Gal. 5:1, 13-18	Luke 9:51-62
Lutheran (LBW)	1 Kgs. 19:14-21	Psalm 16	Gal. 5:1, 13-25	Luke 9:51-62

A primary image in these texts is movement—into the teeth of royal storms for Elijah and Elisha, to Jerusalem for Jesus, and beyond Jerusalem for those who are led by the Spirit. The movement is variously called a journey, a walk, a way, a setting of the face like a flint. The walk behind the plow is arduous, the heat makes the sweat run down your face, and you keep running into boulders. The way is narrow, steep, filled with bandits and hangers-on; it moves through many a wilderness, with long distances between oases, and no *autobahns*; it moves through "fast food strips," with numerous temptations to detour. The food will become scarce, the water will barely slake your thirst, and on many a night you will have no place to lay your head. A stable will have to do.

The interpreter should not soften the claim these texts place upon those who take this journey. No detours or side roads, just straight ahead. No delays, excuses, indecisiveness, or looking back once begun. Even second thoughts are ruled out. Discipleship calls for a decisive break from the past. This is a call for faithfulness and responsibility within relationship. This is a call to stay the course, come what may. But in this walk we are not alone; Christ promises to be with us and lead us along the way. Paul speaks of the Spirit in whose ways we are to walk. If we live by the Spirit, let us also be guided by the Spirit. This way may seem restrictive, with too many constraints on behavior; it may seem too rigorous, with too few rest areas. But it is a way of remarkable freedom, uncommon joy, and an incredible sense of fulfillment.

FIRST LESSON: I KINGS 19:14-21

This pericope starts in the middle of one story (which begins at 19:1) and runs into the next (vv. 19-21). Verses 1-14 will have to be picked up to make sense of this pericope, which centers on the prophetic commission that issues from that encounter with God (vv. 15-18) and Elijah's fulfillment of that part of the commission having to do with Elisha (vv. 19-21). The alternate text from 2 Kings 2 continues the issue of Elisha's succession, at which point Elisha actually picks up the mantle of Elijah and becomes his successor.

In 18:22 Elijah had complained to God that he was the only prophet left who had not bowed the knee to Baal. He was the only true "man of God" left in town—Yahweh's Lone Ranger. This complaint of Elijah is evident in 19:16 as God promises him that Elisha will be his successor, which follows immediately (vv. 19-21). Moreover, God tells Elijah that he is not as alone as he may think; some seven thousand Israelites remain faithful to God (19:18).

We begin with vv. 1-14. Threatened by Ahab and Jezebel, Elijah flees for his life, heading south toward Mt. Sinai, the traditional site of divine revelation. On the way he relives some of Israel's experiences in the wilderness; he complains because of his failures and expresses a wish for death (ironic, given his flight from death at royal hands!). But God again (cf. 17:1-16) provides for life in the midst of death. Having arrived at Sinai, God repeatedly (vv. 9, 13) rebukes Elijah as to what he is doing in *this* place. Elijah, perhaps expecting divine commiseration and focusing on himself, has the same reply (vv. 10, 14): I've been working my head off to no effect; all Israelites have proved unfaithful, and now my life is in danger. It is as if he had heard nothing between the questions. And in fact, while there had been a lot of noise (earthquake, wind, and fire; signs of the storm god Baal but not realities "in" which the God of Israel is to be found), no real communication had taken place. After the noise there was only the "sound of silence." When Elijah simply repeats his reply, God responds (vv. 15-18): Get out of the doldrums, quit the pity party, much work remains to be done, and here are a few starters; besides, you are not alone (see also 18:3-4). No new word was available to Elijah from Mt. Sinai (Elijah was no Moses!); it was essentially the same old word. Nor is Elijah given special protection, only some new particulars and the promise that he will have help to carry out his responsibilities. Hazael and Jehu will be instruments of God's purposes, and a successor prophet will be raised up to continue his work. And seven thousand Israelites.

God's commands to anoint two kings are not actually carried out by Elijah, but by Elisha and one of Elisha's followers (2 Kgs. 8:7-15; 9:1-13). The purpose for making Hazael king of Aram (2 Kgs. 10:32-33) is to cut back Israel's territory and mediate God's judgment on Israel for its idolatry (as God will later use the Assyrians and the Babylonians). The second case

(2 Kgs. 9:1-13) also relates to divine judgment as Jehu puts an end to Ahab's dynasty and initiates reforms that begin to turn back the inroads of Baal on Israel's life. In both cases, God becomes involved in violent human activities, whereby judgment is mediated upon Israel for its unfaithfulness within relationship through a foreign people.

That these commands are not carried out by Elijah himself is striking (Elijah does not even go to Damascus). This ought not be considered disobedience on Elijah's part, but a recognition that God's word regarding the future may have to be adjusted in view of changing circumstances (see 1 Kgs. 21:27-29; 2 Kgs. 22:20 with 23:29). Even more, Elisha does not literally anoint Hazael, but engages in political cunning that enables Hazael to assume the throne of Aram, nor does Elisha actually kill anyone (v. 17). Moreover, the one command that Elijah does carry out (1 Kgs. 19:19-21) does not involve an anointing of Elisha, though his act of throwing his mantle over Elisha symbolically provides for his succession. Such a concern for succession is not the usual way in which prophets are raised up in Israel. Succession is the means God uses in this instance because of the concerns expressed by Elijah and the severity of the crisis for Yahwism in Israel at this time. This crisis calls for continuity in having a "man of God" on the scene who can address the issues forthrightly. This stress on continuity shows that the calling of the prophet as spokesperson of God is the central concern of this narrative.

Elisha (a very rich man) is not eager to pick up Elijah's mantle and begs for a delay to say his goodbyes. Whether Elijah rebukes him is unclear; he appears to tell Elisha to return to what he was doing as if the call had not occurred. Elisha is too indecisive to serve the calling Elijah has in mind. But when Elisha returns home he slaughters the oxen with which he had been working the fields (rather than, say, selling them) and provides a feast for the community; he is given a second chance (unlike Luke 9:61). Elisha's act is a sign that he has made the decision, and that it is irrevocable; he no longer has a vocation to which he can return. Having burned all his bridges, he leaves the farm and follows Elijah, becoming his servant. Elisha actually becomes fully his successor in 2 Kgs. 2:13-14. Jesus acts similarly to Elijah, calling disciples that behave like Elisha, or worse (see below).

Elijah and Elisha exhibit two different responses to God's call, and both remain common among the people of God. (*a*) One is deep discouragement. The work often seems to be nothing more than failure and is at times dangerous to our health, and so we retreat into self-pity or a mountaintop hideaway hoping for a breakthrough word from God that will jump-start our ministry. In Elijah's case, God stays with him and listens to him, but refuses to accept his interpretation of the situation, and commissions him anew for tasks ahead. (*b*) The other is hesitance about becoming involved in the first place, with excuses so easy to cite in an overly busy world. For both kinds of response, the word is that God has decisively entered into the life of the world in Jesus Christ in spite of all appearances to the contrary, has called us to be faithful, sends us out both to trouble the way things are (18:17) and to offer a word that bespeaks new life, and assures us that we are not alone.

SECOND LESSON: GALATIANS 5:1, 13-25

In Galatians 5 Paul shows his deep anger toward those who have disrupted these new congregations in Galatia. He even sarcastically hopes that the knives these people use for circumcision would cut even more deeply (v. 12)! The Galatians were running well (v. 7) until these troublemakers came along. The church itself has become deeply conflicted, endangering its own future (v. 15). Conceit, envy, and provoking one another characterize their life together (v. 26).

Into this dysfunctional situation, Paul speaks a word about freedom (Galatians is called the Magna Carta of Christian liberty). We might be tempted to respond that freedom is precisely the Galatian problem; these people need *more* boundaries, more law and order, not less! But, for Paul, the dangers of returning to slavery through "trying to be justified by law" (v. 4) are greater than the freedom they enjoy in Christ. But Paul also recognizes that this freedom in Christ is both a gifted reality ("Christ set us free") and an objective ("called for freedom"). The freedom *from* slavery to law observance for our justification, becomes a freedom *for* service on behalf of the neighbor (see 1 Cor. 9:19). From within this tension, Paul exhorts the Galatians: do not use this freedom as an opportunity for the flesh; serve one another through love; love your neighbor as yourself; live by the Spirit. The Christian life is defined as "faith working through love" (v. 6) on behalf of the neighbor. Christians fulfill "the whole law" (v. 14) in their love of the neighbor under the guidance of the Spirit (Rom. 13:8).

Those who are in Christ still live in the flesh (= our old self) and hence they will continue to struggle against its wants and its desires. Because of that reality, Christians at times "may not do what [they] want to do" (v. 17; Rom. 7:15). Paul lists the "works" of the flesh as a warning, as that to which the Galatians may succumb to their own future detriment. The law as such does not have the power that the Spirit has in being able to work against such "fleshly" developments within the community.

In their new-found freedom, Christians are to be guided by the Spirit. Paul understands that his exhortations are one means by which the Spirit extends such guidance. To tend to this counsel will have effects in life different from law observance. The law too narrowly circumscribes the shape that life is to take; the guidance of the Spirit leaves life much more open regarding possibilities for love of neighbor. Such openness makes the task of discernment of the needs of the neighbor more urgent, but the potential good is more comprehensive. Moreover, it is not possible to formulate laws that will produce such "fruits." How can laws lead to joy or patience or gentleness? Something more must be at work in people—the Spirit—to lead to such "fruits." It may often be the case that we will be moved by the neighbor's situation to go beyond the law. It may often be the case that we will see that simply to do that which is "legal" may not be moral. It may often be the case that we will recognize that law observance may lead to divisions, while the "fruits" of walking in the Spirit lead to the building up of the community and its flourishing.

Such "fruits" must not now be drawn into a new kind of code for Christian living, as if they constituted a new law. As the effect of the work of the Spirit, these fruits are, finally, the gift of God. Hence the call is to walk in the Spirit, to learn anew to discern how the Spirit may be leading us in ever-new and surprising directions in our walk of faith.

These lists of "vices and virtues" (see Rom. 1:29-31; 1 Cor. 6:9-10) are common in the ancient world; in fact, such "fruits" are found outside the community of faith; non-Christians may know, say, generosity or self-control when they see them, and even practice them. We might speak of the Creator Spirit active beyond the bounds of the Christian community. The difference for Christians may be (but not necessarily) that they are more attuned to the work of the Spirit in them. But the fruits of the Spirit are not somehow automatic or "natural"; those who live by the Spirit also need to be instructed in the guidance of the Spirit. Too many Christians resist the work of the Spirit in their lives (see Eph. 4:30)—and resist instruction!—and hence the gifts are less practiced.

GOSPEL: LUKE 9:51-62

This text (only vv. 59-62 have a parallel, Matt. 8:18-22) begins the next major section of Luke's Gospel: Jesus' journey to Jerusalem (9:51—19:28). The phrase "set his face" is used for the suffering servant and prophet who face opposition (Isa. 50:7; Ezek. 21:1-2). This phrase expresses Jesus' determination to fulfill his mission (Luke 18:31), not a straight-line journey to Jerusalem. But finally there he will be "taken up" (language for Elijah in 2 Kgs. 2:11), a reference to the ascension as the climax of the events to take place in Jerusalem (see Acts 1:22).

In Jesus' first encounter on this journey he is rejected, even though others prepared the way. A sure sign of things to come, he is rejected because of his mission (v. 53), and beyond Jewish borders, as if the villagers somehow could tell. The text focuses on the response of James and John to the rejection; they ask Jesus whether they should call down fire on the city, as Elijah once did (2 Kgs. 1:10). Jesus rebukes them in view of his instruction of 9:5 (see the NRSV footnote to v. 56). This is another way in which Jesus is more than a prophet; his way is the way of the cross, the taking of violence upon himself rather than dishing it out—an all-too-common response of Christians through the centuries (note that 10:12-15 does speak of a *final* judgment).

The story of Jesus' rejection on the way to the cross sets up a story of the cost for those who would follow him along this kind of "Way" (9:57-62), a name for the early Christian movement. This way will entail a cross also for Jesus' followers (see Acts 9:2). One disciple expresses confidence of his ability to follow wherever Jesus leads. Jesus' indirect response lifts up the cost; unlike even the animals, a "home" can never be a settled one for either disciple or master; it will always be on the way (see the Son of Man reference in 9:44). Another disciple requests a delay to bury his father (a tradition; see Gen. 25:9). Jesus' seemingly heartless refusal shows the cost of following him and the priority of that mission over the most pressing of family obligations (the "dead" who do bury are nonfollowers). This response prompts another disciple—who doesn't get the point!—to reply in a comparable, but less compelling way (see the "plowing" Elisha in 1 Kgs. 19:19-21). Jesus' response this time is more direct and sharper than Elijah's: anyone who starts on the way and looks back is not fit for the kingdom of God. No furrow will be straight if those at the plow keep looking back and do not keep their eyes on the way ahead.

Both disciples call Jesus Lord but hesitate to follow where this Lord leads. Calling Jesus Lord is of no account if one's life is not shaped by the cost of staying the course. The end of the way for disciples is not finally Jerusalem, but the kingdom of God. Their journey will extend beyond Jesus' journey, and they will not have the personal presence of Jesus to keep them on course. As the opposition to Jesus increases, so that opposition will not quit when Jesus has been taken up. These narratives reveal this Lord preparing his disciples for that more extended journey.

One must be careful not to soften these demands. Jesus is a prophet whose word is radical, upsetting the normal course of life. One might say that he does not reject family per se, but excuses and delays because of family. One might say that distancing from family priorities enables a more fitting relationship to family. At the least, it claims that so-called "family values" are not the primary values! Even the best of families are too dysfunctional, too permeated with sin and its ill effects, to provide the basic compass point for the shape of the life of a disciple. Only a determined setting of one's face on the Lord who leads us on the way through thick and thin will provide a sure point of orientation; only he has the capacity to hold us on course.

Seventh Sunday after Pentecost
Fourteenth Sunday in Ordinary Time/Proper 9

Lectionary	First Lesson	Psalm	Second Lesson	Gospel
Revised Common	Isa. 66:10-14 or 2 Kgs. 5:1-14	Ps. 66:1-9 or Psalm 30	Gal. 6:(1-6), 7-16	Luke 10:1-11, 16-20
Episcopal (BCP)	Isa. 66:10-16	Psalm 66 or 66:1-8	Gal. 6:(1-10), 14-18	Luke 10:1-12, 16-20
Roman Catholic	Isa. 66:10-14c	Ps. 66:1-7, 16, 20	Gal. 6:14-18	Luke 10:1-12, 17-20 or 10:1-9
Lutheran (LBW)	Isa. 66:10-14	Ps. 66:1-11, 14-18	Gal. 6:1-10, 14-16	Luke 10:1-12, 16, (17-20)

The texts for this Sunday contain no obvious linkages. The image of the harvest in Luke (10:2) is associated with the gathering of dispersed Israelites; this theme would connect well with Isaiah 66, which speaks of the plenitude of the sustenance that mother Jerusalem (God) will provide to the returning exiles. If one takes into account the larger context of Isaiah 66 (vv. 18-23), the mission of the community of faith also comes into view. Also, Isaiah and Luke speak of both judgment and salvation as effects of those who hear or do not hear the word. Paul's word in Gal. 6:9, "let us not grow weary in doing what is right, for we will reap at harvest time, if we do not give up," connects well to the harvest theme in Luke and the urgency of the mission to which we have been called and the energy needed to stay on course.

FIRST LESSON: ISAIAH 66:10-16

These verses from Isaiah have been chosen with no apparent regard for their context; the preacher should make use of the entire literary unit, vv. 6-16. The last major segment in Isaiah (chaps. 56–66; see the study of Isaiah 65 two weeks ago) concerns the fortunes of the people of Israel in the land after their return from exile. The message of the prophet consists of comforting and encouraging words to the faithful, while speaking indictment and judgment to the wicked in the community. In these verses, the judgment is intended for their enemies (v. 5), so this is a word of comfort to the faithful because it promises future deliverance. The words of judgment in this text (vv. 6, 14c-16) bracket the words of specific comfort to the dispirited faithful (vv. 7-14b).

The pericope begins (v. 6) with an announcement about events *within* Jerusalem; God is dealing judgment against the enemy. This prompts a word of hope to the faithful, whose future is likened to a birth and the nurture which follows (vv. 7-9). Birthing and nurturing language is common in Isaiah. In Isa. 26:17-18 and 37:3, Israel is described as being in labor but unable to bring forth children. In Isa. 42:14, God is depicted as the mother who painfully gives birth to a new Israel from the ruins of destruction and exile. In 46:3-4 Israel's God, unlike other deities, nurtures the chosen from the womb to old age. In 49:14-15 God is contrasted with a human mother, who could conceivably forget her nursing child, but God (as nursing mother) will never forget. This text also speaks (vv. 19-21) of an incredible reality: the land is full of children! The question is raised as to where all these children could come from in view of the fact that Israel was bereaved and barren. The implied answer is that the children have come from God; God has given birth (42:14) to these children and reared them. This theme is picked up again in 54:1-2; Israel (or Jerusalem) is personified as a barren woman, who will have children but never be in labor.

These texts inform our passage; Jerusalem is personified as a mother who has given birth, but quickly and painlessly, without any labor. Incredible! God's rhetorical questions in v. 9 refer back to vv. 7-8; God, having begun the act of creation, would complete the birthing process, and the children will not want for nourishment (vv. 10-14). Any who still mourn over Israel's destruction are called to rejoice (note the emphasis upon joy) with Jerusalem over all the newborns and to nurse from her full breasts. The image of nursing continues in v. 12—the river and overflowing stream are images used for the abundant milk that the mother has to provide. Verse 13 should come as no surprise, given the other passages in Isaiah; mother Jerusalem (mother language is also used for the church) and mother God come together. God is like a mother who provides Israel sustenance through the nursing mother Jerusalem. The word *comfort* is used three times to stress the effect upon a dispirited people. This language is, of course, metaphorical (similar to God being like a father; Ps. 103:13), and provides a powerful image of God who brings to birth and nurtures the children with such abundance. Some might find it difficult to think of God as one who gives birth and nurses the child at the breast. But to ignore such images is to neglect a powerful resource for speaking of God. Mother language for God provides an image of unequaled power for certain dimensions of the divine–human relationship; what other language can convey as fully the nearness and tenderness of God, namely, the child in the mother's womb (no other human experience conveys such closeness) and nursing at her breast?

Verses 14-16 speak of the effects of this divine work, and for the children at least these words would be heard in positive terms. On the one hand, the divine sustenance will lead to growth and healthy bodies (literally, bones—

an interesting link to milk!). On the other hand, God's hand will be against the enemies of the children. Strong images of fire and sword are used to depict the divine anger against those who seek to harm the children. Such images of judgment are sometimes difficult for moderns (and perhaps led to the elimination of vv. 15-16 in the pericope!). In seeking to interpret such images, the reader might think of a mother bear and her cubs or of human mothers, who speak of their fierceness when it comes to protecting their children.

These images present themes of both creation and redemption. Israel (to use the image of dead bones from Ezek. 37:1-14) needs to be re-created, to be born anew, and to be nurtured with blessings. This divine work affects not simply the spiritual life, but catches up the physical and the material. Even the vision of eternal life includes the resurrection of the body in a new heaven and a new *earth* (note the earthly new world in Isa. 65:17-25). Moreover, Israel is delivered from forces that enslave it socially, politically, and economically. Babylon is defeated; Persia adopts policies that enable Israel to return to the land and to function well there. We are wise if we think of both creation and redemption in holistic terms as the work of a God who seeks life, health, wholeness, and the flourishing of community. God is one who provides milk that not only makes your heart rejoice but your bones strong (v. 14).

SECOND LESSON: GALATIANS 6:1-16

In this final segment from Galatians Paul continues what he began in chapter 5—drawing out the implications of God's act in Jesus Christ for Christian living. Paul emphasizes Christian responsibility for the upbuilding of the community; Paul is less concerned at this point about issues of individual spirituality.

The freedom of the gospel and life in the Spirit mean that the disciple is to steer clear of two ditches. First, this freedom ought not lead to a new centering on the self. This could take the form of self-indulgence (5:13; 6:8) such as those "works" listed in 5:19-21, or the form of "a good showing in the flesh" (6:12), any self-promotion regarding one's relationship with God; in fact, the disciple is now free from having to worry about such matters. Second, freedom from the law does not mean less responsibility for the neighbor; indeed, the entire law has now been gathered into one, focused on the neighbor (5:14). This open-ended commandment makes responsibility for others more comprehensive than does any body of laws. Love of neighbor can never be circumscribed in a list of laws, for lists cannot comprehend or anticipate everything that the neighbor might need from us in life's ever-changing circumstances. The disciple has always to be alert to ways—from small gestures to major contributions—in which love for neighbor can be practiced or promoted. In this ongoing task of discernment, the disciple grounds any specific response in the gifts of the Spirit (5:22-23).

At the same time, Paul obviously believes that good counsel to the Christian who has received the Spirit is in order (6:1). For all the gifts we receive, instruction is still needed. Sowing "to your own flesh" rather than "to the Spirit" (6:8) is a lively possibility for even the Christian. This counsel is understood as a discerning of how the gifts of the Spirit could take on flesh in daily circumstances. Paul offers several such words of counsel in chapter 6, which include encouragement and warning. He no doubt has in mind the particular Galatian context (see 5:26), but his words can prompt our imaginations regarding applicability across any life situation. How might these gifts of the Spirit come to life in our everyday worlds, so much more complex than Paul ever imagined? We are invited to extrapolate along the grain of Paul's interpretation of the gifts and see how we might show them forth in our own time.

One gift of the Spirit is gentleness (5:23). This gift can take on flesh when a transgressor is restored to the community (6:1; cf. Matt. 18:15-22). It stands over against a judgmental approach to the *repentant* sinners in our midst—everyone will stand in need of such an approach at one time or another. This statement needs to be put together with the stinging rebuke in Paul's letter.

Another gift of the Spirit is self-control. Paul warns that those who seek to restore in gentleness could get caught up in a comparable transgression (6:1). We can be deceived (6:7), and Paul has self-deception in mind (6:3). Paul warns that God's moral order functions in such a way that our actions—whether to the flesh or to the Spirit—will be returned upon our heads. The choices we make do count and will have effects for good or for evil.

Another gift of the Spirit is kindness. This can be shown specifically in situations where a person has burdens too great to bear alone (6:2-5; see 5:13). His appeal to the "law of Christ" may refer to 5:14. But Paul warns that we ought not think so highly of ourselves that showing kindness becomes an occasion for boasting in our kindness: Thank God we are not as bad off as they are, and how kind we are! If this were to happen, it would be self-deception, for we have no grounds for such a claim. Then *we* would become the burden! Self-examination ("testing") becomes key to sorting this out; if there is to be pride, let it be in what we *actually do* on behalf of the other, not in what we think about those who have become burdened or about ourselves because we have been so kind.

Another gift of the Spirit is generosity. This can be demonstrated in supporting our teachers in the faith (6:7). We could extend this counsel to include others who have contributed to our life and well-being in one way or another.

In vv. 9-10, Paul gathers the entire list of gifts of the Spirit and speaks of them as doing what is right and working for the good of all whenever we have opportunity. The upbuilding of the community, especially the Christian family, is to be the focus.

The final verses of Galatians gather the main points that Paul wishes to make. Obeying the law—circumcision is the focus, but we could add any law—can never be a reason for boasting. We can only boast in what Christ has done, most supremely on the cross, for the salvation we receive is a gift wrought by that work, not our own obedience. Boasting in Christ is a form of praise, a witness before others. Boasting in our own obedience deflects that praise away from Christ. The effect of Christ's work is a crucifixion of the world—the flesh with its passions and desires (5:24) has been nailed to the cross; we who are in Christ now live by the Spirit. And this new life is a new creation (2 Cor. 5:17), a reality that refashions the world. This "new creation" which is "everything" is further defined in 5:6 as "faith working through love" (see 1 Cor. 7:19, where it includes obeying the commandments).

Paul does not end his letter as he began. He concludes with a blessing upon those who are faithful (defined here as the new Israel), which contrasts with the word of rebuke and curse at the beginning (1:8-9). Paul's word about his own suffering for the sake of Christ is a word of candor that opens up such a possibility for any who would follow in the way of the cross.

GOSPEL: LUKE 10:1-12, 16-20

Only Luke has two stories of Jesus' commissioning disciples; they are similar in focus and show the importance of mission for Luke. The first describes Jesus' sending of the Twelve, imbued with authority to proclaim the reign of God, to cure diseases, and to exorcise demons (9:1-10). The disciples are given instructions, proceed to carry out the mission "everywhere," and report back to Jesus all that they have done. This Sunday's text uniquely speaks of the mission of the Seventy, called to prepare the way in towns Jesus was visiting (10:1). This group moves the commission to mission beyond the Twelve, in effect calling *all* who follow Jesus. The number seventy probably recalls the seventy nations of Genesis 10, anticipating a worldwide mission. For Luke, mission was not simply that which Jesus generated as he was leaving (Luke 24:47; Acts 1:8); it was integral to his entire ministry. Jesus' own mission is a paradigm for Christian mission.

The Seventy are given essentially the same commission as the Twelve and they report back to Jesus regarding their success. The instructions Jesus gives obviously cannot be transferred literally to every age; strategies for mission are shaped in view of specific situations. Yet, they do give direction; Christians are invited to extrapolate along the basic grain of each instruction to see how it might continue to apply. Generally, the strategies are lean and to the point; they keep the disciples on the move, not lingering long over rejection or wasting energy in active resistance. They are to be lambs, not wolves; vulnerably present, not on the attack. The most basic tasks are to extend a word of peace, not threat, to proclaim the nearness of the kingdom of God, and to heal the sick. The disciples are to travel light (modified in 22:35-36) and be dependent upon the hospitality of others. They are to eat what is put before them, not be fussy about diet or food laws. Given the urgency of the task, they are not to stop and chat along the way. The peace they are to extend is more than a pro forma greeting (see 24:36); it signals the salvation they bring. Through their word of peace, salvation will become an effective reality in the hearts of those who are responsive. But that word is resistible; those who are not open to the word of peace will not receive it. But the disciples are not to adjust the message to see if it might become more acceptable; they simply move on with the same basic word.

The reason Jesus gives for the mission has become a classic missionary text (10:2; see Matt. 9:37-38). The image of harvest has its roots in God's gathering of scattered exiles (Isa. 27:12); God will return them to their own land with its center in Jerusalem (see Isa. 66:6-16). The prophets understood this gathering in eschatological terms, so the harvest also has reference to the end times; like the harvest, the kingdom of God is near (vv. 9, 11). The image is one of urgency. The grain in this image does not have to be planted or cared for; the disciples' task is to harvest what is already mature, given God's long-standing work in Israel. In contemporary terms, God has long been active among all peoples of the earth preparing them for the harvest. Our task is to make connections between that comprehensive work of God and the specific word about Jesus, to name the God who has been involved in people's lives before we showed up with the Bible in our hands. We do not bring God anywhere; we go where God has been long at work.

Moreover, the grain to be harvested is plentiful; God's work in the world has been richly effective, though not apparent to normal vision. These bountiful effects of God's activity mean, however, that many laborers will be needed to bring in the harvest. Indeed, it is striking that Jesus asks the Seventy to pray to God for more! They are not enough to do the job. This prayer, which may reflect an early Christian petition, remains pertinent in every age. Disciples are always needed to gather in those whom God has touched. God has chosen not to farm alone! This work is urgent. The grain is ready to harvest, and the kingdom of God into which the harvest is to be gathered is at hand (v. 11).

Jesus then moves to another rural image (10:3). Disciples are like endangered lambs; the mission to which we are called places us at risk in a perilous world. We will encounter opposition from many sources wherever we go. To be lambs means that we are not to be like wolves! The wolves may refer to false teachers (Acts 20:28-30; Ezek. 22:27; 34:1-10) or to any who do not receive them (v. 10); but they are dangerous and on the attack. But we are not to return in kind or pass judgment (vv. 10-11; see 9:51-56). We are only to wipe the dust of those towns from off our feet and announce to those who have rejected what they have missed (v. 11; see 9:5). Their refusal entails not only the rejection of the messenger, but—and this is scary—a rejection of Jesus and the God who sent him (v. 16).

The verses not assigned in the lectionary (vv. 12-15) make clear that God will see to the judgment; that is not the business of disciples. The woes of vv. 13-15 against cities in Galilee suggest that significant levels of rejection have already occurred (see 9:53); this may be both an assurance to the disciples and a statement of the seriousness of the response people make to the word that they bring. The unfavorable comparison to the Gentiles in Tyre and Sidon is sharply worded, and recalls the words of the prophets against the chosen (see Amos 3:2); the closer the relationship, the worse the effects of brokenness if it occurs.

But some people do listen to the disciples, listening to whom is to listen to the word of Jesus (v. 16). The Seventy joyfully report that in preaching that word of Jesus even the demons listen! But Jesus' response does not reinforce their joy. They are not to stress the results of their mission. Satan's "fall" was already assured before their work began; they are in effect cleaning up after the key battle has been won by God. Moreover, the power they do have over evil (symbolized by snakes and scorpions; Ps. 91:13) has been given to them by Jesus; because of this, the powers of evil will not be effective against them. And so, they should not engage in self-congratulation at the effects of their mission, but rejoice that their names have been entered into the register of the kingdom of God (see Matt. 7:22-23).

Eighth Sunday after Pentecost
Fifteenth Sunday in Ordinary Time/Proper 10

Lectionary	First Lesson	Psalm	Second Lesson	Gospel
Revised Common	Deut. 30:9-14 or Amos 7:7-17	Ps. 25:1-10 or Psalm 82	Col. 1:1-14	Luke 10:25-37
Episcopal (BCP)	Deut. 30:9-14	Psalm 25 or 25:3-9	Col. 1:1-14	Luke 10:25-37
Roman Catholic	Deut. 30:10-14	Ps. 69:14, 17, 30-31, 33-34, 36-37	Col. 1:15-20	Luke 10:25-37
Lutheran (LBW)	Deut. 30:9-14	Ps. 25:1-9	Col. 1:1-14	Luke 10:25-37

Whether to obey the law is an issue all of us, Christian or not, face every day. But just as important is how we *interpret* the law. Do we obey the posted speed limit, or do we fudge because we know the police will allow us five to ten miles over the limit? Do we state exactly what we gave to church last year on our tax forms, or do we exaggerate a little because we know the IRS won't bother with small amounts? If we choose the latter in either case, we *interpret* the law as having a built-in fudge. Do we thereby (like the lawyer) seek to justify our actions? We may not think we are disobedient since we have interpreted the law in a certain way. From another angle, we may be meticulous in obeying the law, and would not think of overstepping the boundaries. We will drive the posted speed limits and pay every last penny of the taxes we owe. Yet, this is interpreting the law as well and, in so doing, we may forget that laws are often open-ended. For example, what specifically is entailed in honoring your father and mother, or loving your neighbor as yourself? To be truly obedient to such laws often entails great sensitivity and imagination that cannot be reduced to a legal formulation (who is my neighbor?); or going beyond any specific law (does killing mean only not putting someone to death?); or recognizing that to obey one law we may have to disobey another (the dilemma of the priest and the Levite). And, then, if we have to choose, how do we know which law to obey?

In both ways of thinking about the law Jesus' question becomes pertinent: "What do you read there [in the law]?" You know the law, now how do you interpret it? Seeking to discern what it means both to obey and interpret the law is a complex issue. These texts provide an occasion for exploring some of this complexity.

EIGHTH SUNDAY AFTER PENTECOST/PROPER 10

FIRST LESSON: DEUTERONOMY 30:9-14

This lesson begins midsentence in several translations (see NRSV). Deuteronomy 30:9-14 is part of a larger unit that includes the entire chapter, though a major break comes between v. 10 and v. 11 and marks a shift from words about a future time to those directed more specifically to those standing before Moses.

While this text is set in the time of Moses, the Babylonian exiles are the likely audience (see "as is now the case" in 29:28). They are wrestling with the realities of exile—apostasy, fear, distress, and wondering about the continuing validity of God's promises, not least the promise of the land. Verse 1 shows that vv. 1-10 pertain after the fall of Jerusalem and the exile. The reader is to recall Deut. 4:25-31, which demonstrates that even in exile, God "will not forget the covenant with your ancestors that he swore to them." The Lord will not forget this promise, no matter the nature of the people's response. Verses 6-10 envisage a future for Israel when God will give them a new heart, and obedience and faithfulness will follow naturally (see Jer. 31:31-34; Ezek. 36:26-28). With their new heart, they will "turn to the Lord God with all your heart and with all your soul" (v. 10); after they have returned to the land God will make them prosperous, and take delight in doing so (v. 9). This delight of God shows that God's involvement in the relationship with Israel has a deeply emotional dimension. What happens to this relationship matters to God.

Verses 11-20 move back to the present, to the people standing before Moses. Moses assumes that obedience to "this commandment" is possible; a community of life and well-being can be created in the land of promise. "This commandment" (singular) probably refers most basically to the commandment to "love the Lord your God" in Deut. 6:5 (see Deut. 11:22; 19:9), from which will flow obedience to other commandments. Verse 20 speaks of this commandment in highly personal terms as "loving the Lord your God, obeying him, and holding fast to him." What is at stake is a personal relationship to God, not an impersonal subscription to a list of codified rules and regulations. Paul in Rom. 10:6-10 applies this text to the nearness of righteousness that comes by faith.

This faithfulness to God to which the people of God are called is not out of reach or unclear or something for which they have to search. This word has been proclaimed clearly within their hearing and they themselves have spoken these words in worship; it has become a part of who they are. This word is not a hidden wisdom that only the initiates in some esoteric cult can discern. This word is not a list of regulations that only lawyers can interpret. This word is not an idea that only those with great intelligence can figure out. This word is not some form of spirituality that only deeply religious types can grasp. This word is a clear, straightforward word for all, regardless of age, gender, or class, regardless of level of learning or station in life or status in the community: You shall love the Lord your God with all your heart and soul and might. The choice before these already chosen ones (v. 19) is to be faithful to the God who has called them into the covenant relationship within which they presently stand. And such fidelity means "life to you and length of days" (v. 20).

The choice of being faithful to God looks easy, and the text says as much. Yet, several texts in this section of Deuteronomy subvert that confidence with notices of Israel's inclination to infidelity (29:17-28; 30:17-19; 31:16-20; 32:15-35). The people are called to obey, and indeed they often can, but they are also so deeply inclined to disloyalty that they will not finally be able to control their own future or create the order the law suggests they can. Deuteronomy ends by leaving readers with uncertainty: What might be in store for this inevitably disobedient people? This ending does give some basis for hope (29:10-15; 30:4-10; 31:1-8; 33:1-29); a sense of expectancy is generated by these texts. But it is qualified by a realism regarding the human condition, so that the people of God must ground their hope, not in their strength or capacity for obedience, but in the promised presence of God and the certainty of divine faithfulness. It is only because God goes with them and keeps promises that they can be strong and courageous and can be assured that the promises will be fulfilled.

This sense of Deuteronomy's ending, like the Word of God more generally, is a two-edged sword for Israel and for us. We can count on the divine promise and God's word being near us, but our fears in the face of uncertainty and death, and our inclination to disobedience, raise questions about participation in the promise. The way into the promised future is only possible if God is at work, not only in us but also beyond us and in spite of us.

SECOND LESSON: COLOSSIANS 1:1-14

Colossians reads as if it were written by Paul, but it was probably the product of a disciple who addressed a controversy in the Colossian congregation similar to that faced by the Galatians. The question is whether Christ's redemptive work was complete or whether certain practices—in private piety and public worship—had to be undertaken to bring that work to full flower (2:16-23). The letter's basic response to the conflict is to make certain claims about Jesus Christ, appropriating the language used by the false teachers (particularly cosmic themes) and the wisdom tradition (for instance, Proverbs 8). The letter's high Christology emphasizes the "fullness" of Christ's relationship to God and the centrality and sufficiency of his death and resurrection

EIGHTH SUNDAY AFTER PENTECOST/PROPER 10

for the salvation of the entire cosmos. *All* things have been reconciled to God through Jesus Christ. This gospel needs no supplementation by pious practices; those who suggest otherwise detract from the person and work of Christ and from the freedom to which believers have been called.

The lectionary text consists of an introduction similar to letters of Paul: a greeting (vv. 1-2) and a thanksgiving stating the principal themes of the letter (vv. 3-14). The thanksgiving, with its commendation to faithful Christians, suggests that the congregation has not yet yielded to false teachings and the writer continues in prayer for their steadfastness in the faith. This emphasis upon commending the saints—their faith, love, bearing fruit, comprehension of the grace of God—is worthy of attention by preachers. Such commendation is a relatively uncommon practice. The reason for this may be rooted in a desire to reserve praise for God. But the writer's example should be followed more often, not least because challenges to the faith are increasing and the temptation to nonchalance is severe. Christians do need to hear words about themselves other than sin and salvation. The saints are valued members of the household of God (an important theme in Colossians) and should be publicly recognized as such. Their steady and energetic participation is integral to the health of the household. Their faithful work makes a difference regarding the future of the Christian movement; it makes a difference to God.

The references to prayer for the saints is another theme that could be sounded more often. Note the language: "we have not ceased praying for you"; Epaphras is "always wrestling in his prayers on your behalf" (1:3, 9; 2:1; 4:12). This entails both praying for them and telling them they are being held up in prayer. Such a word encourages them in their service and in their own life of prayer. We know how important it is in human relationships to be told we have been remembered; it is no less significant in our relationship with God. In turn, the saints are encouraged to devote themselves to prayer and to pray for their leaders (4:2-3).

The bold claims about Jesus Christ include language with trinitarian overtones; God is the Father of Jesus Christ, Christ is "beloved Son," and life "in the Spirit" describes one who is a "minister of Christ." This language will be filled out in the Christ hymn that follows; in Christ "all the fullness of God was pleased to dwell" (v. 19). At the same time, this focus in Christ does not lead to diminishment of God the Father. To be centered in God is important for the Christ hymn, perhaps so that the writer cannot be charged with a kind of Christomonism by his opponents. It is God's will that he is an apostle of Christ. The greeting is only from "God our Father" (without the usual addition of "and the Lord Jesus Christ"). Only God the Father is addressed in prayer and thanked (vv. 3, 12). The grace of God grounds the gospel (vv. 5-6) and God the Father is the one who has "rescued us from the power of darkness" and enabled us to share in the inheritance of the saints (vv. 12-13). A key objective for the saints is to "be filled with the knowledge of God's will" and to "grow in the knowledge of God" (vv. 9-10). The not-uncommon notion that Jesus came in order to save us from (the wrath of) God cannot be grounded in this letter. God the Father is the author of our salvation and works through Jesus Christ to reconcile all things to God (1:20).

The notes of a familiar triad are sounded in the opening verses: faith, hope, and love (see 1 Cor. 13:13). The faith of the Colossians in Christ Jesus shows itself in love for all the saints because of the hope of eternal life (v. 4). These themes are played out in the verses that follow. The word of the gospel of truth has been bearing fruit among the Colossians "in every good work" (vv. 6, 10) as it has throughout the world. But growth and maturation themes are also sounded, especially growing in the knowledge of God and of the divine will (vv. 9-10; see 1:28; 4:12). The knowledge of God is not attained once and for all; there is always more to learn about God. In fact, the more we know about God the more of a mystery God becomes. God is not demystified through our growing understanding, and God becomes more interesting the more we search and inquire. Perhaps the church is often dull because it has ceased to be an exploring, probing church, and has been satisfied with treasuring what it has already put in the bank. Jesus promised to send the Spirit to lead us into all the truth and we have not yet arrived.

The Colossians have come to "fullness in Christ" (2:10), but need to "be filled with" spiritual wisdom (see 3:10); an existing relationship needs to be developed if it is to prosper and bear good fruit. Such an understanding is also important because we need to be "prepared" to face difficult times (see 1:24). But in such times we will also need the strength that comes from God and the patience to endure whatever is thrown our way (v. 11). But, even then, we should be joyful and grateful for all that God has done for us through Jesus Christ. The text ends in a virtual litany of this grand work of God: we have been enabled to share in eternal life; we have been rescued from the powers of evil; we have been transferred from a darkened home to one that is full of light; we have been redeemed; and we have been forgiven. For all this we should indeed be filled with joy and thanksgiving.

GOSPEL: LUKE 10:25-37

This parable is unique to Luke; vv. 25-28 have parallels in Matt. 22:34-40 and Mark 12:28-34. This text should be linked with the Gospel text for next Sunday. The primary point of comparison is probably the Good Samaritan and Mary. Readers in that culture would not expect to see them in the positions they occupy. Yet, in some respects, the *lawyer* is like Mary—asking questions, listening to Jesus' teaching, engaging in dialogue. And the Samaritan is like Martha—doing what needs to be done if the neighbor is to be well served (whether the robber's victim or Jesus himself!). The interpreter should not demonize the lawyer or Martha, let alone the priest and Levite. The preacher might also think of different ways for the hearers to see that, at one moment or another in their lives, they might find themselves in the shoes of *each* character in both texts.

The dialogue of questions and answers was a rabbinical method and so the "test" probably does not have a malevolent purpose. The upshot of the dialogue is that Jesus and the lawyer (a teacher of the Torah, one of the wise in 10:21) do not disagree about the law or about what must one do to inherit eternal life, but they do disagree about how to interpret the law. "What do you read there?" It may be disarming that Jesus' response to the question about eternal life is an appeal to the law rather than to faith. Note, however, that the commandment cited has first to do with a loyal relationship with God (from Deut. 6:5); one is to love God with every fiber of one's being (even the mind, the one phrase not found in Deut. 6:5). The lawyer combines the commandments from Deut. 6:5 and Lev. 19:18, showing that they had been linked prior to Jesus' time. This combination is implicit already in Deut. 10:12-22.

The lawyer's next question is stated in such a way that some might not qualify as neighbor; "who" implies less than everyone. The narrator informs us that the lawyer asks this question to justify his action; he has in mind a definition of neighbor that informs his obedience and he wants this to be confirmed by Jesus. Unlike the lawyer, Jesus recognizes that the definition of neighbor in the context of Lev. 19:18 is comprehensive, including the poor, hired hands, the deaf, the blind, one's own kin, and the aged. It includes not only "*any* of your people" (19:18), but "you shall love the *alien* as yourself!" (19:34). Even aliens are neighbors! Leviticus excludes no one. That may be why several texts regard Lev. 19:18 as the summation of the law of Moses (Rom. 13:9; Gal. 5:14).

Jesus' parable of the "good" Samaritan is an illustration of the comprehensiveness of the levitical law. In other words, Jesus appeals to the lawyer's own law to make his point! In effect, Jesus tells him that to place restrictions on the identity of neighbor is to violate the law which he himself holds dear. For Jesus, knowing the law is insufficient; one must interpret it correctly. If the lawyer wants to know what it means to obey the law of the neighbor he must read Leviticus right. As Jesus asks, "What do you read there?" (v. 26)! Jesus emerges as the true lawyer here, the true teacher of the Torah; he lays no other claim on the lawyer than that which was integral to his own tradition. If the lawyer does the law so interpreted, Jesus says, he will live (v. 28). And so will the dying neighbor who now comes into view in the story.

But, having interpreted the law aright, what might it take to obey this law? The story could make an obvious point: the dying man is so clearly a neighbor in need that no reason could be advanced for not reaching out to him. But this makes it too easy for the Samaritan; if helping the man is so obvious a move, why would he stand out as an example? Would that it could be said: *anyone* would help such a person! We know from our own situation in twentieth-century America where, say, millions of children languish in poverty, that the Samaritan's move to help is not so obvious. People, good Christian people, have their reasons, perhaps even good reasons, such as "I may get sued if I help." The priest and Levite state no reasons for passing the man by, but we can be sure they have their reasons. And what might they be? Because they are identified as a priest and a Levite, and not just any passers-by, their identity as religious leaders and interpreters of the law (and hence hold positions comparable to the lawyer) is important.

We return to our question: What might it take to obey the law of the neighbor? It may mean that, in order to obey this law, we may have to disobey other laws. To put the question differently, what makes the Samaritan "good"? And what do the priest and the Levite do that places them under judgment? The key issue seems to be that, upon seeing the victim, the Samaritan gives priority to the law of the neighbor. The priest and Levite have their reasons and obeying more particular laws may be a key factor, for example, purity laws prohibiting the touching of dead persons (Lev. 21:1-3; Num. 19:10b-13). Whether they considered it, or acted reflexively, a decision was made not to obey the law of the neighbor. Perhaps because the law about corpses was so clear, while the neighbor law was more open-ended and not so specific, it allowed for an escape; they (like the lawyer) could be selective about who a neighbor was. They did not recognize that the law of the neighbor had been elevated within their own tradition to a place of priority among the laws.

Commentators often note that the Samaritans are neither Jew nor Greek, but a kind of half-breed people, both ethnically and religiously (see John 4:9). A point regarding such an alien being the one to help the victim of random violence is certainly in mind for Luke. Not as often noted is that both Jews and Samaritans had the law in common (the truncated Samaritan canon included the Pentateuch) and a good Samaritan lawyer may well have answered Jesus' question as does the Jewish lawyer. In any case, the

Samaritan is confronted with which law to obey as much as the priest and Levite. And the Samaritan chooses the law of the neighbor rather than another law that might restrict access to this dying person. What makes the Samaritan "good" is his capacity to discern which law has priority in this crisis for the neighbor. Jesus commends the Samaritan's way of reading the law to the lawyer. Jesus commends his way of reading Leviticus! The choice of what law is to be obeyed in a given situation will at times be presented to everyone within the community of faith. The law is clear: You shall love your neighbor as yourself. Jesus' question to each of us is this: How do you read?

Ninth Sunday after Pentecost
Sixteenth Sunday in Ordinary Time/Proper 11

Lectionary	First Lesson	Psalm	Second Lesson	Gospel
Revised Common	Gen. 18:1-10a or Amos 8:1-12	Psalm 15 or 52	Col. 1:15-28	Luke 10:38-42
Episcopal (BCP)	Gen. 18:1-10a, (10b-14)	Psalm 15	Col. 1:21-29	Luke 10:38-42
Roman Catholic	Gen. 18:1-10a	Ps. 15:1-5	Col. 1:24-28	Luke 10:38-42
Lutheran (LBW)	Gen. 18:1-10a, (10b-14)	Psalm 15	Col. 1:21-28	Luke 10:38-42

The theme of hospitality centers the texts from Genesis and Luke (and Colossians' theme of reconciliation is an extension of this). Modern culture presents numerous challenges to the practice of hospitality—acts of benevolence toward those outside one's circle of family and friends. We live increasingly isolated lives, seldom reaching beyond a close circle. We live in a self-protective age where parents must warn their children about strangers; who knows what might be lurking beneath a kind and gentle facade? So, hospitality today entails some risk in moving toward the stranger, with less than full certainty as to how we might be received. This uncertainty has carried over into our life of worship, a setting in which hospitality should be practiced in premier ways. And if we do not practice hospitality in that setting, might we be less than hospitable to the God who appears among us in the "least of these"?

These texts involve hospitality toward God and Jesus, not simply other human beings. Such hospitality is not only a spiritual matter but a response of the whole self. While God's presence in the midst of life remains hidden, God does assume flesh and blood in the neighbor (Matt. 25:43-45), a text where lack of hospitality is grounds for judgment. Hebrews 13:2 stresses its importance, for "some have entertained angels without knowing it." Generally, hospitality is commended to all (see 1 Pet. 4:9; 3 John 5–8).

FIRST LESSON: GENESIS 18:1-10a, (10b-14)

This story depicts an appearance of God to Abraham, with which Sarah becomes involved. When God earlier promised Abraham a son, with Sarah designated as the mother for the first time, Abraham had responded with incredulous laughter (17:15-22). In this text the birth announcement is repeated so that Sarah overhears (vv. 9-15); she also responds with laughter. This combination of hospitality and birth announcement is also present in 2 Kgs. 4:8-17, another text appointed for this Sunday.

Verses 1-8 set the issue as one of hospitality extended to strangers. Verses 9-15 retain an interest in hospitality, with their focus on Sarah's *reception* of the birth announcement. Issues of hospitality relate to receiving others and the words they may speak, in this case the words of God. From the narrator's point of view, Yahweh appears to Abraham (v. 1); from Abraham's point of view, however, three men stand near him (v. 2). Yahweh has assumed human form and is included among the three men; the other two are angelic attendants (so 19:1). Abraham to this point is not aware of these identities, so the reader knows more than he does; his hospitality is not prompted by a desire to please God. Sarah's response also must be interpreted with this in mind. Abraham's hospitality follows a servant's protocol: honoring, inviting, refreshing, preparing, serving. Haste language appears five times. He gives of his best and is concerned about their welfare.

The guests' question and promise in vv. 9-10 disrupt the reception. The reader will remember (from 17:16-17) that Abraham expresses the same incredulity and asks essentially the same questions as does Sarah, who is listening "off-camera" (18:12-13). Both have a hard time believing the promise. Promises were as hard to believe then as with us today, living as we often do with broken promises (from partners to politicians). We are tempted to reply: promises, promises! Our reasons may be different today, but they are also based on life experience, and the incredulity is as real.

The narrator inserts a word about age (v. 11), as if to provide an objective view on Sarah's own comments; the issue for her is no longer barrenness. The question in v. 13 inquires of Sarah's laughter. If it is an accusatory question, then it claims that Sarah should know better than to laugh, for nothing is too wonderful for God. More likely, the "why" is designed to continue the conversation. This is suggested by God's inviting paraphrase of Sarah's question, omitting references to age. The question of v. 14 is also a genuine question, designed to move Abraham and Sarah beyond their limited view of the future to a consideration of God's possibilities. Then v. 10 is repeated, as if to make sure the promise remains clear in light of the intervening conversation.

God seeks a response from *Abraham* about Sarah's laughter. This may be due to his not having told Sarah about the events of chap. 17; if so, he is as much to blame for Sarah's response as she is. Abraham now remains silent, but Sarah does not (v. 15), though hers is a voice "off-stage." Her denial (v. 15) could be a lie or an attempt to withdraw her laughter, as she is more aware of the situation and the probable identity of the speaker. But

God says it remains a fact (though does not pass judgment). This keeps both Sarah and Abraham on the same level regarding the laughing reception of God's promise. Sarah's incredulity is typical for such announcements (see the Shunammite woman, 2 Kgs. 4:16; and Mary, Luke 1:34), as is the "due time" reference (2 Kgs. 4:16). This twice-stated reference finds its fulfillment in 21:1, where God visits Sarah "as he had said." God's explicit action enables Sarah to become pregnant, yet Abraham's paternity and the normal time for gestation are not set aside. The end of this segment seems incomplete; the intent may be to leave the reader (and Sarah and Abraham) in a state of some uncertainty as to what the future will bring.

The precise meaning of the word *pele'*, translated "wonderful" or "hard" (v. 14), is uncertain: competence (Deut. 17:8), or ability to accomplish something (Jer. 32:17), or something marvelous (Ps. 118:23). The related plural noun can refer to God's wonderful deeds (Exod. 3:20). The question itself is also difficult; no simple yes-or-no answer is possible. If yes, then we could delimit in a specific way what is possible for God. If no, then God's freedom is so elevated that God's gift of *genuine* power to the creature is lost (Gen. 1:28); moreover, what is possible for God must be consistent with who God is. The text does not claim that God alone has power, or that God's power is irresistible, but that God's promises will not fail. God will find a way into the future of a promised son in spite of the seemingly insurmountable hurdles of bodily limits and uncertain human responses. No situation can *finally* stymie the divine purposes. New Testament texts that use such language (Mark 10:27; Luke 1:37) need to be considered with other texts: Matt. 17:20 (nothing is impossible for faithful *human beings*); Matt. 26:39 (Jesus' prayer, "*if* it is possible"); and Mark 6:5 (where Jesus' powers of healing are limited by the nature of the situation).

A text such as this calls for sentences in which God is the subject. God makes the promised future possible. God is the source of hope in situations where the way into the future seems entirely blocked off. God gives shape to possibilities when everything in life seems impossible. The engagement of God amid the problems of daily life opens up the future rather than closing it down.

SECOND LESSON: COLOSSIANS 1:15-28

This text consists of two major segments, a hymn about Christ with implications (vv. 15-23) and a commendation regarding Paul's interest in the Colossian congregation (vv. 24-28). The latter is not actually concluded until 2:5. The Christ-hymn (vv. 15-20) is commonly considered to be an older hymn, perhaps from an early Christian liturgy (as Phil. 2:6-11). The Colossians may have known the hymn, so the author may use familiar language to ground his argument regarding Christ. Against a "low Christology" put forward by false teachers, the hymn supports the author's claim regarding the centrality and sufficiency of the work of Jesus Christ for the salvation of the entire cosmos.

The emphasis in the hymn on "all things" stresses that nothing in all creation (including cosmic powers important to the false teachers) stands outside of Christ's creative and redemptive work. The hymn makes five claims about Jesus Christ that are cosmic and comprehensive in their efficacy and scope. These claims present an opportunity for the preacher to give an overview of the Christian confession regarding Christ. A typical congregation will include many who cannot articulate the significance of Jesus Christ very well and could use such a review. Given the centrality of the church's confession regarding Jesus Christ, we should return to such reflections on a regular basis.

First, Christ participated in creation (vv. 15-17). In a manner not unlike the claims for the Logos in John 1:1-3, Christ was involved in the creation of all things, including all cosmic and earthly powers. This is not simply a claim that Christ is "before all things," but that all creation continues to be held together by his ongoing work in creation (v. 17). To speak of Christ as the "firstborn of all creation" does not mean that Christ was a created being, but that he is superior to everything in all creation. Unlike human beings, Christ is not created in the image of God, but *is* the image of the invisible God. This material is dependent upon the wisdom tradition in Prov. 8:22-31 (the text for Trinity Sunday, see above). The claim is that Christ's relation to creation is indispensable for speaking about Christ as redeemer. Without the creational claims, the word about Christ's redemption will be: (*a*) less well grounded (redemption presupposes a creation to redeem and a Creator whose love and purpose extends to all); (*b*) more anemic with respect to the fabric of its significance (it has a bodily, earthly dimension, not just a spiritual import); (*c*) and more narrow in efficacy and scope (Christ's work has a universal, indeed a cosmic significance and effect).

Second, Christ is the head of the church (v. 18a). Extending the Pauline metaphor of the church as body (1 Cor. 12:12-27), Christ is the head of the body (see Eph. 1:22-23), indeed of all things (Col. 2:10). As the head is related to the body, Christ is the ruler over the Christian community, without which it would not exist or function. Indeed, growth in the body is possible only because of Christ who is the head (2:19). The kingdom (1:13), in which Christ reigns over its subjects, is another metaphor used for the church.

Third, Christ was raised from the dead (v. 18b). Christ is not simply the first of those raised, but as the risen one he rules over the church, indeed over all things. Fourth, God was incarnate in Jesus Christ (v. 19); 2:9 stresses that God dwelt *bodily*. The "fullness of God" theme seeks to prevent any understanding that this indwelling of God was only partial or was only an emanation from God. Fifth, through the cross all things were reconciled to God (v. 20; 2:13-14). *God* is the subject of this reconciliation, and hence the claims that can be made regarding it. The scope of God's work in Christ is not partial, but universal—including not simply earthly creatures but cosmic powers. The effect of this work of Christ is "peace" throughout the entire cosmos. Nothing in all creation constitutes a threat to the salvation that Christ has wrought; the powers have been disarmed (2:15).

Verses 21-23 bring the importance of this confession home to the readers ("you"; "now"). They were estranged from God, thinking and living in ways that were opposed to God's purposes. Because of what Christ has done, they can be presented before God the judge and declared blameless. At the same time, faithfulness to the God of this gospel is not an option (v. 23). Verses 24-28 begin to speak of the apostle's role in making this confession regarding God's work in Christ known to all the world, with the objective of "presenting everyone mature in Christ" (v. 28). This role is laid out in ideal fashion and so it could inform the understanding of others so engaged. The task of making known this "mystery" entails preaching and teaching "in all wisdom." The language of wisdom (see 1:9) implies that these activities of interpreting and proclaiming are to be informed by careful discernment regarding the situation to be addressed and maturity in the knowledge of God's will.

The apostle's role also entails suffering (1:24), but the significance ascribed to that suffering is difficult to discern. Given the claims about Christ elsewhere, it does not likely mean that Christ's redemptive work is incomplete. The phrase, "for the sake of the church," suggests that the ongoing task of building up the church will entail suffering on the part of those so engaged. Christ's sufferings do not end the suffering needed for the growth of the church. Such missional suffering is not to be understood in terms of retribution or a masochistic search for suffering. Suffering "goes with the territory" of mission. In so enabling the growth of the church Christ's suffering is "completed."

GOSPEL: LUKE 10:38-42

This text (only in Luke; see John 12:1-3) is closely related to last Sunday's Gospel (see above). There a lawyer seeks to limit which neighbors he is obliged to serve; here Martha suggests that there is so much work to do that everyone ought to be as busy as she. There a lawyer has trouble doing—he always has another question to ask, another conversation to have; here Martha has trouble listening—she always has something more to do. It is as if Luke wants to correct a misconception that could arise from a too-critical view of the lawyer, as if only doing counts. Or, Luke wants to protect against a too-critical view of Martha, as if only learning and listening count. The reader should keep the Samaritan and Martha together, as well as Mary and the lawyer. Together, the stories present a balanced perspective.

If this balance is maintained, then the common criticism that Jesus puts down women who have chosen to focus on serving and doing is somewhat allayed. Jesus does have a critical word for Martha, not unlike the word Jesus speaks to the lawyer. The word focuses not on the activity per se, but on the concern for self it exhibits ("worried and distracted"), as if this were a way in which life could be made meaningful (see 10:29). From another angle, a problem arises when we make Jesus' word to Martha into a generalization, as if that word were applicable in every time and place. We may have times when an imbalance in doing and listening arises. We may need to receive Jesus' word to Martha in some situations; at other times we may need to hear his word to the lawyer.

Even so, does not Jesus prefer Mary's way over Martha's? We may make several responses to that question. First, we recognize the unusual scene of a woman sitting at Jesus' feet; she is portrayed as a disciple, like the women in 8:1-3 (see 23:55-56; 24:22-24). In that culture the master's feet is for male disciples. This may have been an important point to make about the inclusive character of those disciples who follow Jesus.

Second, we recall that, during Jesus' ministry, a basic duty of disciples was to listen to Jesus teach, as in the following text (11:1). For Jesus' time on earth, the best thing for a disciple to do was to listen and learn from him. For this time, Mary's way is the "better part," the "one thing" that is needed (this could be a more general reference to Jesus' word—rather than food—being the only matter of ultimate concern, see 4:4). Would Jesus have put it to Martha as he did if he were always going to be around?

Third, we note the key role Luke gives to serving elsewhere; indeed, Jesus himself takes on the role of servant (12:37; 22:24-27; see Mark 10:45). So Martha's "many tasks" (= "much service") stands directly in line with Jesus' own self-identification, which becomes a paradigm for a disciple's identity. So, finally, it may not be Martha's service per se that is the issue, but a certain lack of focus that she brings to her tasks.

Finally, we return to the note of hospitality. Comparison with the Genesis story could bring insight. With Sarah and Abraham, God appears incognito; they entertain angels unawares. With Martha and Mary, Jesus is a known presence from the beginning. God can encounter us in both ways, at times hidden beneath the mundane ("the least of these") and at times when we know we have to do with God. We need to be prepared for both kinds of encounter. Moreover, as with God's entry into the life of Abraham and Sarah, Jesus' presence in Martha's home occasions disruption, an unexpectedness in the conversation that leaves folks somewhat uncomfortable, not knowing whether to laugh or cry. That is at times the way it is with God. Also, both households do well on the service end of hospitality, putting out the red carpet for the guest. But the hospitality may not extend to the words spoken by the guest, and the guest may have to speak a critical word. However welcoming we may think we are, God has a word to speak that deserves careful attention. Will we be hospitable to that word? Even though it disrupts the normal routine of our lives? Even though it takes the form of a seemingly impossible promise?